MY GENTLE WAR
(MEMOIR OF AN ESSEX GIRL)
by
Joy Lennick

My Gentle War (Memoir of an Essex Girl)

Copyright © Joy Lennick 2012

ISBN 13: 978-1480066632

ISBN 10: 148006663X

ALL RIGHTS RESERVED

Published by WordPlay
wordplayenquiries@mail.com
wordplaywritersforum.blogspot.com

ACKNOWLEDGEMENTS

My sincerest thanks to Ian Govan and Michael Barton of WordPlay for their help through the publishing process and to WordPlay for publishing my memoir. Also, to Maureen Moss, my editor who has an eagle eye. Finally, my thanks to my good friend, Jean Wilson for her constant encouragement.

My Gentle War (Memoir of an Essex Girl)

In loving memory of my parents Lila nee Havard and Charles Mansfield, Aunt Sal (Sarah Jones), Aunt Flo (Florrie Palmer), and to all the kind people who took in evacuees in World War II.

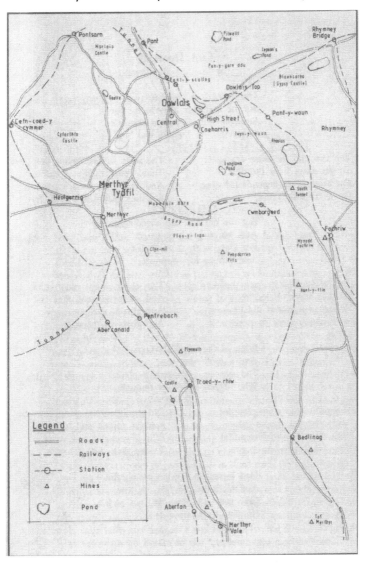

Merthyr   Tydfil

CONTENTS

PROLOGUE

MANY DECADES HAVE PASSED since I spent treasured time on Mountain Hare, in the midst of a small, close-knit, intriguing, friendly – dare I say 'nosey' – community, sleepily looking down on bustling Merthyr Tydfil, in South Wales. Much clichéd, time, of course, does not stand still for a second. Indeed, as the years multiply, it seems to spin like a giddying, gaudily colourful tin top from my childhood, inducing my pen and computer fingers to faster speed, so onward I must go.

Drawn by the Welsh blood in me via my maternal grand-parents and forebears, I have always been inquisitive about my 'Welsh half's' history. In an eye-blink, mist wreathed, forbidding, grey-black slag tips materialise, as does my miniscule whilst enchanting, mysterious wood: *Pencoedcae.* It emerges from beneath its present, unforgiving concrete blanket, as green, lush and magnetic as when I tentatively explored it (wary of ghosts of Druid priests, ancient warriors or the Welsh dragon itself).

Dylan's 'bible black, sloe black' Wales is woven from a rich, hardy material, softened by its much lauded, ubiquitous choirs and sheep-dotted abundant acres of verdant countryside. It is a broken jigsaw that lingers in my head begging reassemblance.

Except for some personal tragedies - which occur in most lives - over the years life has been mostly kindness itself, but whatever has befallen me, my early 'Welsh adventure' has been there on the periphery, impatiently waiting in the wings, waiting

8

for me to start digging – to start unravelling the tangled wool ball of my childhood and my family's history. The perpetual question hovers:

'Where to start?'

'At the beginning, of course!'

Always that annoying bit of advice. But exactly *where* do *our* Welsh Havards begin?

HISTORY OF THE HAVARDS/ HARVARDS/ HOWARDS

IT HAS BEEN AUTHENTICATED that a certain *Sir Walter Havard,* whose French name was *Walter Havre de Grace (circa 1090)* settled in Wales. However, the name of *Havard* was originally of Norse (Norwegian) origin and means *High Steward,* a common first name in contemporary Trondheim – an area from where the Dukes of Normandy and Earls of Orkney originated: its origins possibly from Norse mythology. Recorded in the Norse Sagas is a *Thornstein Havardson* who was a "great chief "on Sanday in the Orkneys. Havard is still a common surname in contemporary Normandy, notably connected to the well known *Havard Cornille* Foundry, which cast the Liberty Bell to commemorate the Normandy Landings of June 6th 1944.

 Sir Walter Havard was a Norman Knight and was given the Manor of Pontgwilym, near Brecon by *Bernard de Neufmarche de Lions* who lived in the area on a farm. Around 1093, several barons and knights built a strong castle the north side of the Usk,near Brecon. One of these was *Sir Walter Havard*, who, with these men, destabilised the Norman frontier with Wales against the wishes of William the First and William the Second. Three of the knights were *Sir Humphrey Ffergill, Sir Miles Piegard,* and *Sir John Waldebieffe.* Memorable names indeed!

 Later, the Havards became integrated into Brecon society and contributed to their credit, becoming one of the most powerful families in the County of Brecon. Several Havards are listed amongst the aristocracy and landed gentry in Burke's Peerage (contemporary). However, according to the Norman system, a first son inherited everything. Other children often became impoverished and disappeared from recorded history, more's the pity. This is probably where our branch of the Havards came from! Hey ho.

In the 13th century, the Havards founded the Havard Chapel in what is now Brecon Cathedral. It is the Chapel of the Prince of Wales' own regiment, formerly the Regiment of Wales. A certain *Thomas Havard of Caerleon* in Gwent was present at the Battle of Bosworth in 1485 – a battle which established the Tudor Dynasty. In the 16th Century, *Joan Havard* was born near Brecon and her father was *William Havard of Tredomen.* The Havards were probably bilingual and were Catholic recusants.

A well known variant on the name Havard is *Harvard. The Harvards of Stratford Upon Avon* were friends of the Shakespeare family and Harvard House in Stratford is a half-timbered Tudor house open to the public. This house belonged to the mother of *John Havard* who founded *Harvard University* in the United States of America in the early 17th century.

Howard – another variant of Havard – is the family name of the Dukes of Norfolk. *Thomas Howard,* Duke of Norfolk and Earl Marshall, was a minister of Henry V111 and uncle to both the unfortunate Anne Bowllyn and Catherine Howard. Thomas was sentenced to death by Henry V111, but fortunately for him and unfortunately for the King…Henry V111 died the day before the execution was due to take place, and according to custom, the duke was released. Unusual in the court of Henry V111, he lived to an old age.

My less illustrious - though not to me - maternal grandfather *Samuel Havard* was born in 1884 and lived at 26 Spring Street, Dowlais, near Merthyr Tydfil. He married *Sarah Jane Phillips* of Pwyllywiad (Duckspool) situated above Mountain Hare and Merthyr town. He was a House Carpenter (Journeyman). My grandparents married in November of 1905 and my mother Lila, named after a fairy queen Grandma saw in a play - while Elizabeth appeared on her birth certificate – had *Hair like fine-spun, brown sugar* - Grandad later poetically said, was born in October 1906. They had three further daughters: *Peg (Margaret) A pretty girl; Mattie (Martha) With a coal-black head of hair,* and *Edna, A sweet but ailing child,* (who nevertheless lived until she was seventy-nine). They also had one son, John. *He was the apple of Grandma's eye and spoiled something rotten as a child,* Mum confided. Sadly, he was only to see half a century.

I have discovered over the years that serendipities do occur from time to time. For instance, while becoming increasingly fascinated by the Havard genealogy, my husband met a character actor in London by the name of *Dyfyd Havard.* They got chatting, and interested to learn that my mother was a Havard, he telephoned me. Our conversation was enlightening -

I'm appearing in "The Corn Is Green" at the National Theatre, perhaps you   would like to bring your mother along and we can meet up for a drink after the performance, he suggested. Would we?! The stage play - which also featured Deborah Kerr – was absorbing and thoroughly enjoyable, and as arranged, we met Dyfyd in a nearby bar. We could hardly have missed him for he wore a cherry red, roll neck sweater and a megawatt smile. Of short to medium height, he was topped by a thatch of snowy white hair. Charm exuded from every pore, and my mother in particular was delighted to meet him. We kept in touch for a while and a family friend promised to send a copy of the family tree. However I never received it. Dyfyd gave me the names of a few more relatives to contact in the Islington area of London: one a very elderly man who was in a retirement home. Two others were "Doctors of Letters" but I had no reply to my very polite letters from either gentleman. Methinks some people are needlessly suspicious of an ulterior motive, like avarice!

During this period, Dyfyd retired to Fishguard in Wales and I didn't hear from him again. I would like to think of him still performing on that great stage in the sky, fanciful thought.

My next connection with the ancient Havard family was via Brecon Cathedral, where the Deacon was most helpful. Sadly, just before my visit to Brecon, my beloved mother, Lila nee Havard Mansfield, died aged 82. How fascinated she would have been to have discovered that a distant cousin of hers was one of the former Bishops of St. David's Cathedral. I know that I was.

However tenuous the Havard-Harvard-Howard link-up to our particular branch of the family, it's been most interesting learning about the history of the names.

IN THE BEGINNING

The 1930s

'We could never have loved the earth so well if we had no childhood in it.'

George Eliot, 1860

NINETEEN-THIRTY-TWO WAS not, by all accounts, a good year in which to be born. Not that I had a choice in the matter. And, judging from a report in the Romford (Essex) Times of January, 1932, the previous year was an equally inopportune time for even the most minor population explosion.

"Unwept, unhonoured and unsung, 1931, which will pass into history as one of the grimmest years since the close of war, stumbled away into the outer darkness from countless widely opened doors on Thursday night."

But then, apart from air conditioning being invented, Amelia Earhart becoming the first woman to fly solo across the Atlantic and scientists splitting the atom...the thirties were also to become infamous by countless terrible happenings. The fact that a certain Adolf Hitler became the Chancellor of Germany in 1930 was to prove ominous, not only for Germany itself, but for the whole world. Later in that era, there was the Hindenberg disaster, Japan invaded China, and the Spanish Civil War began. History, not satisfied with that doom-laden list of disasters, added the opening of the first Nazi concentration camp, the abdication of King Edward V111 (hardly on a par with

15

the former evil happening) and Hitler's annexing of Austria. It was, of course, completed by the declaration of World War 11 in September of 1939.

Being a mere sprog at the time, the above couldn't fortunately even enter my consciousness, although it was to effect my future, along with that of most of the inhabitants of the planet. Despite the poor economic climate, and doubtless due to the ignorance and misconceptions (no pun intended) about sex prevalent at the time, I was only one of many mouths to feed. For while high moral standards were publicly called for, it is open to conjecture as to how many 'premature' babies were born to the recently wed in the twenties and thirties. *Eight pounds? Goodness what a whopper for a six month baby!* Supposedly helpful suggestions circulating, such as - *Drink a glass of water straight after...* and *Do 'it' standing up...* (I have it on good authority) were tried by many, and to their chagrin, found wanting. Mum never did reveal which one of us four was born after the water 'antidote'...Early condoms were hardly featherweight: *Like washing your feet with your socks on,* it was said.

With no real understanding or yardstick against which to measure our daily experiences, and blessed with caring parents, we three children, brothers Bryan Charles aged one and Terence John aged three, with me being the eldest at five (in 1937), jogged merrily along, ignorant of what was happening in the wider world. Walking to school was fun, for Dagenham village (we had moved there from Rush Green), still pretty in places, boasting some thatched while sagging cottages, was a friendly, peaceful place.

Once past the corner, smelly wooden slaughterhouse building (nose pinched tightly), which marked the start of the village, it perked up as I approached 'Arfy's' (Arthur's) bakers, with its seductive aroma of freshly baked bread and rolls wafting magnetically out into the street. The manager of the Co-Op – emitting odours of sawdust and Bovril - (the shop not the manager) sometimes waved en route. And once in school – a small, cosy building, the other side of Dagenham church and the Cross Keys public house - a very old inn said to have secret tunnels beneath its floors leading to the church opposite, I was as happy as a lark. (The said tunnels were used by religious persons fleeing persecution at various times in history, as well as the odd highwayman, including - it was claimed - the infamous Dick Turpin.) I learned to count on a colourful abacus, wrote simple words in sand on a tray, or with chalk on a small blackboard, before progressing to an exercise book and reading about the adventures of Brer Rabbit and his friends. Chosen to play the triangle and shake the tambourine in the school band, my cup ranneth over. 'War' was a foreign country and just a three lettered word.

One of my most vivid recollections from the 1930s, is of Dad making giant silver and gold crowns and checking red, white and blue bunting, plus writing on large banners (he was a dab hand at calligraphy) for the Coronation party of King George VI and Queen Elizabeth in the May of 1937. Doubtless Mum, equally capable in a different way, assisted with the making of the assorted cakes and jellies. The prospect of a street party was spine tingling then. A first for brother Terry and me; Bryan being too young to absorb it all. We were overawed at the sight of the sheeted tables groaning under the weight of lots of desirable, edible goodies. Portraits of the new King and Queen held court over all, everyone was jolly; and clutching souvenir mugs and bags of sweets to our chests, we returned home with different stories.

Dad, of course, remembered a very different Dagenham, and while it seemed fine to us children, he said it was a far cry from the pig rearing, potato and pea-cropped pastoral place of previous years. *Such unimaginative progress,* he thought. The green fields of his youth were turning to a dull, orangey-red, but whilst eschewing too much change, and except for the war years and several holidays abroad, he remained in Dagenham throughout his life.

Prior to the war, and sometimes during and just after it, life was difficult for many, and when Dad was occasionally on 'short hours' before and at the end of World War II, we too had to put 'Shreaded Wheat' box soles in our shoes now and then – more especially the boys as they were harder on their footwear. Mum said that the

Foolhardy and pretentious clung desperately to their foxes, musquash or beavers, and there was a saying then: *She's all fur coat and no drawers, that one!* At one stage, she felt the downslide personally as she had to pawn her engagement ring, and to her deep regret, never had it back. Luckily, however much our modest fortunes wavered in uncertain times, we were blessed with caring relatives, the paternal side of the family having more financial clout.

Apart from his Air Force years, Dad remained a Lighter-man ** on the River Thames all his working life, and stayed firmly and unwaveringly on the bottom rung of the ladder, content with his lot. He expressed the belief that *Promotion means more work and responsibility and more hours away from home!* And home was his absolute castle. Mum - patient, feminine as Spring, unselfish and easy-going - was the perfect antithesis of him. Dad didn't suffer fools gladly, was stoic and capable, had an earthy sense of humour like his father, was intelligent, and called a spade a spade - while having endless patience for his various hobbies – and he adored Mum. He was as solid as the Rock of Gibraltar. Mum was also harmlessly flirtatious, great fun and careful with her money (the Depression had left its mark), if not her love. They were an excellent foil for each other.

Home life was eggs and bacon spluttering, and crumpets toasting to the accompaniment of 'Hutch' on the piano, his dark brown voice booming forth from the wireless; or the plaintive tones of singer Al Bowlly (sadly later killed in the Blitz). I recall being fond of The Ink Spots too, especially their 'Whispering Grass.' Now and then we listened to Carol Gibbons and the Savoy Orpheans, playing in the background while we amused ourselves with board games; the boys sometimes playing more innocent war games, with not a spot of blood spilt. Sunday summer noises echo down the years - pea-pods popping (eager fingers for that job), gem-like marbles clinking in the hallway, the sound of Dagenham's church bells prodding the undecided or lazy, irritating the atheists; the rattle and whirr of the lawn-mower; the aroma of beef roasting. My mind's eye also sees Mum doing a cheeky rumba to Edmundo Ross as she lays the table for lunch ('dinner' on a Sunday). Home was also a brown rexine suite - leather just out of reach – the settee of which became more and more elevated as the week wore on. Mum (think of Laurie Lee's 'Cider with Rosie's' mother) had a habit of secreting 'things' under the cushions day by day - hair scarves, hair curlers, magazines, newspapers, wrapped half bars of chocolates, or sweets, which seemed to multiply as the days increased as if some sexual-like shenanigans were at work. Sometimes - I used to help 'de-elevate' said settee on Saturdays when older - I would find Mum's second best, 'bubble-gum-pink' lace-up corset, careful of its painful wires or bones. Now and then, she'd come home from shopping or work, and, peering around, asked, *Are the boys in or out?* After assurance that were out, she would whip off her torture chamber with a huge sigh of relief and shove it under the cushions to join the said 'pile.' Despite the discomfort, she would urge me to *Wear one, Joycee, you could catch a cold!* when I reached my teens. *NEVER!* I vowed, and never did.

Having introduced me to the silver screen with the advent of 'Snow White and the Seven Dwarfs' (the witch invoking nightmares), Mum and Dad further treated us children to a brief holiday in Southend-on-Sea, where we stayed at a B & B boarding house, which smelled strongly of boiled cabbage mixed with lavender lino polish; in sight of the Gasometer. We paddled in a cold, grey sea but thought it wonderful...

The Kursaal Fun Fair had us goggle eyed, but the piece de resistance for me was Snow White's Cottage complete with Snow White and the Seven Dwarfs at the Westcliff Playground. To complete the delights, there was a replica of Shirley Temple's bedroom in Hollywood on Southend Pier. I watched most of her films in awe. Mulling it over, perhaps our parents were looking to the future, and not liking what they saw, arranged a last minute holiday, for who knew if we would all survive the war?!

** 'Lighter-men' worked hard transferring goods between ships and quays aboard flat-bottomed barges called 'Lighters' in the Port of London. (I would sometimes hear the eerie fog-hooter warning at night when curled up in bed like a ball and would wonder how Dad was, trapped in that icy cold, all-enveloping grey shroud.) He would later reassure me and say that he was, *As right as nine- pence, eating eggs and bacon and playing cards.* But of course, being on or near the busy river at night, especially when foggy, was fraught with danger and I overheard him telling Mum that: *We fished another poor sod out of the water last night!* on more than a few occasions. Inebriated souls, chancing their uncertain way along narrow, often slippery, muddy river banks, imbibed more than the 'golden stuff' before their lives ended. There is a Watermans' Hall in St.Mary at Hill, Billingsgate, London dating from 1780 and it is the only surviving Georgian Guild Hall.

OUR MINI ACRE

EVERYTHING IN OUR GARDEN was lovely before the war started. Well, almost. Death belonged, naturally, to the insect or avian world and the sun passed behind a cloud when we discovered a fledgling with a limp neck and no future lying in the strip of alleyway edging the back fence of our garden, under a plane tree. Death's more encompassing shadow was too soon to show itself as the war gathered pace. It must be said, however, that our garden was a limited playground, to be treated with respect. No ball games were allowed then, only maybe "catch," which fell short in the excitement department. It was, however, a peaceful oasis and a safe harbour, for we were not allowed to play outside its confines, my two brothers and I being under the age of eight.

Narrow, elongated mini-acre that it was, our garden was planted with much forethought and tended with meticulous care by our Dad. Surely nobody else's fingers were as green – although it took us a while to fully understand the description – for they looked pinky/brown to us! The dictates and needs of each season were vigorously heeded and bowed to, and woe betide the heavy footed. When I beheaded a row of soldier straight tulips, aged two, Mum said that Dad scorned me for the rest of the day!

From the back step of our semi-detached, modest house - the sky a ribbon of blue/grey between us and the Jinks ("Butchers") family next door - our eyes delighted in a rainbow of flowers and an array of lush plants, bushes, plus some fruit and vegetables: our teepee runner bean contraption proving an interesting addition. The loganberries, pregnant with juice, and hugging the back fence promising saliva-inducing crumbles and pies, were a further plus.

It was easy to be fanciful in our small plot, for so much grew there which was evocative of other places, other people. Heavily scented stocks and scruffy, leggy wallflowers of Grandad Mansfield; London hospital, and the unpleasant smell of ether and rubber sheets (ugh). Also the slimy, smelly stalks and dripping 'watering-can-tap' in old Dagenham cemetery, where Mum's beloved sister, Mattie (Martha), lay since dying of tuberculosis at the tender age of seventeen, the year I was born. In that graveyard too were buried one of Mum's best friends 'Lylie' who had died young in childbirth, and three tiny local children burned to death in a shed after playing with matches - their trio of matching, miniature stone crosses forever etched in my head. Mum and I were regular visitors to place flowers on their graves. This last tragedy featured as a salutary lesson in my young life as it made me terrified of fire and aware of the dangers, which wasn't a bad thing. A few stately white lilies graced another corner of our smothered plot, putting me in mind of the Lady of Shallot and other maidens, with hands crossed upon their still bosoms, seen in some book or other, or reminiscent of prone effigies in our local church. Sweet and heady mock orange blossom conjured up flying confetti, strains of organ music and clouds of tulle, for wedding watching at Old Dagenham church was a short-lived favourite pastime. Yet another part of the garden was ignited by a burning broom bush, and bright daisies nodded agreeably behind clusters of sooty-black and regal purple and brown pansies traced with vibrant yellow, brightening the path. 'Pongy' geraniums offended the nose but pleased the eye, and a multi-ballerinaed fuschia tree danced in its tub, while large marigolds punctuated the earth like oversized, bronze full stops. There too, were delicate, pastel hued sweet peas, fluttering on green strings like captive butterflies, and cornflowers hardly the colour of corn, mingling with foxgloves and delphiniums which could compete with the bluest summer sky and my brothers' eyes. Not forgetting the vivid purple lupins with their interesting, furry seedpods. When Dad wasn't around, we relieved the 'Aunti'- rrhinum or snapdragon as we sometimes called it, of one or two of its strange blooms, for they could swallow your little digit whole or you could manipulate their 'mouths' and do a comic turn if you had a mind to. *"Pieces of eight"*, or *"What's the time Mr Policeman?"* At times, there was a profusion of pinks and carnations, but roses, Dad's overall favourites, were more prolific. My maternal grandfather Samuel Havard, walked the three miles from his house in Becontree on many a Sunday morning to choose a suitable rose for his buttonhole before stopping off to: *Wet my whistle!* in the Dagenham Working Men's club, thence home a tad happier for his Sunday roast. In every delicate shade, Dad's roses trailed from and smothered fences, some with petals fully uncurled, open to the sun and any insect that cared to call, some neat and complete, budded and half-closed like miniature umbrellas, or fully blown and fading. Many were more fragrant than Woolworth's perfumery counter.

Our garden was a little bit of heaven, and gave our whole family immense pleasure, until we were told to dig a dirty great hole in the centre of the lawn and one of the rose beds for the erection of an ugly 'Anderson' shelter that is. Stoic as ever about the urgent, sensible need - although many were later killed sheltering within them, fortunately not ours - I wouldn't mind betting that Dad's eyes watered a bit on the day he took the spade from the musty shed. But, before that awful day, we three children shared the delights and disappointments that combine to incorporate the ordered chaos that is Nature . Younger brother Bryan, or his senior Terry, would thrust their noses between many a slug and me with a wondering '*Cor*!' and push a probing stick in holes which promised many legged or winged creatures, more commonly worms, to see how it all worked. Uncaring, happy as a pig in a sty, Bryan especially sat in many a muddy spot before being whipped off by Mum for a needy bath. Older brother Terry was just as curious, and I can recall him collecting tiny frogs and suggesting 'frog races' which were erratic affairs as frogs didn't seem to know about straight lines! Like most children, we also erected tents and made simple camps on the lawn from old sheets and blankets (when playing cowboys and Indians or Tarzan and Jane), had plain spitting or cherry stone spitting competitions, and the boys later swapped cigarette cards, which they threw with vigour down the lawn. (Sports figures were particularly popular, especially cricketers and footballers, as were royalty and film stars.) One time I had to be rescued from the enthusiastic hands of a female playmate/future doctor, when she stuck a pencil in my navel in an attempt to 'operate' and take out my appendix!! The rougher, 'survival' attitude and world of the street kids was still a few years away. Can more maturely experienced 'wonders' ever match those early, innocent discoveries? What a creation of nature was the colourful ladybird: *Flyaway home,* or a delicate, ethereal dragonfly.

Having to leave their beloved house and garden must have been a wrench for both my parents, and I can only imagine what sad thoughts filled Dad's head as he locked the front door and visualised his bountiful mini acre disappearing under a mile high mass of weeds as mother nature did her worst.

Even from this huge chasm of time, I can actually recall a couple of friends shouting out *Good Luck! a*s we closed the front gate, prior to leaving for South Wales. One of them – an almost snowy-headed lad called Terry O'Neil, lived opposite me. We had often walked to school together. As an adult – well suited to his gentle, kind nature – Terry became a Minister of the church. At one stage, as I grew older, his mother expressed the wish that we should marry, but we remained platonic friends until our lives meandered down different paths. I would have made a most unsuitable Minister's wife! He found an ideal match: a young woman, pretty and as dark-haired as he was fair.

I nurtured the memory of two, heavenly scented, lilac trees in bloom at each gate post, but of course it was September so they couldn't have been. The 'Truth' - or our perception thereof - wears many guises.

THE UNCERTAIN THIRTIES

LIKE AN INDECISIVE LOCUST – thankfully - the Depression only hovered over us, and the 'wolf' never bared its fangs in our front doorway. Unfortunately, another wolf in disguise, whilst equally not on our doorstep, was soon to affect our whole family's peaceful existence. This was to prove a far from novel situation, for soon every family in the United Kingdom was to be affected in one way or another.

In Germany, the machinery of war was being oiled, but experiencing the tunnel vision of the very young, we children were more aware of our creature comforts and what was happening in our immediate environment. To us 'ominous sounds in the wings' meant only thunder And so, while brother Bryan practiced drawing a *Tiger Moff* and Terry assembled his Meccano into some weird contraption, our Dad - Charles Edward Ernest Mansfield – a Lighter-man on the River Thames, as has been mentioned; like two of his brothers and their father before them, joined the Royal Air Force Reserve in May, 1939. A keen diarist, he noted the important event:

Joined the RAF. Twelve days training at Markham, Norfolk Job in workshops. Thirty-five minute flip in Wellington – VERY GOOD! Rained for nearly two days…

I wonder, did he have an inkling that war would be declared within four months, or was he taken in, like so many others, that the United Kingdom would remain a wary friend of warring Germany? Dad had already had a taste - albeit a brief one - of war as an Air Force cadet in the last part of World War 1. There was a sepia photograph of him with straight back, legs bound, and serious-faced, in the photo-box. He admitted to flying in his imagination on clear, moonlit nights but remained grounded, which was just as well as the Sopworth Pups, et al were delicate structures prone to crashing then, and was spared duty and the horrors of serving 'abroad'.

SEPIA DAD – CIRCA 1918

A blue-serge-clad, fresh-faced youth:
'broom handle' back,
swaddle-legged –
standing "at ease" proud –
gazes at me unseeing,
from his sepia world.

His eyes are filled with
anticipatory excitement as he
flies in fancy with the stars by night -
gazes with ardent longing
on the winged air-borne phantoms
silhouetted against the moon.

No clairvoyant messenger
foretold the future.
How could he have known that
in but two decades
he would again experience the horrors of war;
be captured for posterity in similar stance?

29

The burning question remains unanswered:
What to do with tyrants?
A dichotomy…
Could genetic engineering one day hold the key?!

Whatever Dad did or didn't think about the current situation, being in the Air Force Reserves - blue fortunately his colour - he was one of the first men to be mobilised in 1939.

The historic meeting between Prime Minister Neville Chamberlain and Hitler in Berchtesgaden in 1939 and the fact that the scales were tipped on the side of evil, escaped my notice, as my nose was probably in some book or other or I could have been in the garden making 'flower cakes.' With no feelings of foreboding of a doom-laden future, the summer days of that year passed by unremarkably enough. Stories about Dick and Dora appealed; sums were getting harder. And every day there was some new discovery on which to wonder. A morning, diamond-studded spider's web, was magic to us children, as was the process of a tadpole turning into a frog. What magic stuff was frogspawn!

And then, quite suddenly, everything was topsy-turvy; everything changed. The simplicity of our childhood was threatened by an unknown, mysterious 'something.' Dad noted in his diary – quite succinctly – what that mysterious 'something' was:

SEPTEMBER, WE ARE AT WAR WITH GERMANY

9TH Leave. Arrived Dagenham at 12.50 a.m

Left for Merthyr Tydfil at 3.40 p.m. with Lila and the kiddies until Monday 12th. And then?

And so a new, slightly nerve-wracking, exciting phase in our lives began.

THE JOURNEY

Paddington station was a seething mass of humanity - predominant colours khaki and varying shades of blue - as brothers, husbands, fathers, sons and boy friends either kissed their loved ones goodbye or boarded trains with them. We were, fortunately, in the latter category as Dad had leave until the 12.th Precious little time but a bonus, especially for Mum, who was so much more aware of what the future *could* hold. On the station platform, people hugged tighter than usual. I had never seen so many tears shed in one place before…Hankies fluttered like anaemic bunting as trains steamed out of the station. Bemused by so many tears, we children nevertheless jingled the 'holiday money' in our pockets for 'evacuee' was still a strange word and a foreign concept to us. We were not 'tagged' (that would come later in the war) but obediently carried our gas masks over our shoulders. At first, in our confused minds, especially Bryan's, Clacton or Southend (former Shangri Las) lay, sun-kissed and sandy at the end of those snaking lines. He clutched his own little case, which he had packed and repacked himself, doubtless wondering why he couldn't include his bucket and spade. But, while Merthyr Tydfil, South Wales, land of my mother, has mountains and hills aplenty, it has no golden beaches.

For his part, Terry, shy and ill at ease, stood as close to Dad as he possibly could, like a third limb. Still in holiday mode, we had to be calmed as carriage doors slammed, reverberating down the length of the platform, our noses reacting as the smoke belched from the train's funnel. A guard blew his shrill whistle, a blood red flag whipped the air, and - like a huge, fat and speedy caterpillar - we were off. Apart from a few, subdued strangers, our train compartment contained our quieter than usual parents and three bubbly children, later bent on visiting 'the little room' as frequently as they dared (peeing on the railway lines held a certain fascination). Red-eyed, our Mum bit her nails (a habit when worried). *Let's know when you are up to your elbows, Lila,* Dad used to say. Dad was stoic and primed for action in Air Force blue, his cap at a jaunty angle over dark hair, sleeked flat with Brylcreem.

Handsome as Valentino, without the smouldering eyes... his mother maintained. Dad tried reassuring Mum:

Of course our house will still be there when we return, darling, he said, optimistically. Mum returned to the topic several times, whilst we children couldn't quite get our heads around the concept of our house *not* being there. The realisation, actuality and awful aftermath of bombing was yet to come.

And so we clattered on, swallowing up the miles, carving up fields and scattering sheep. We passed tiny back yards and lines of pee-free nappies, tea-free tablecloths and floppy, legless sundry school greys flapping in the breeze. As the journey progressed, our train's side and door windows – acting as a delightful triptych of ever moving natural paintings - captured the essence of the countryside, offered us more abundance of variegated greens, tinged with early autumnal hues, than we had ever seen! Framed and fragmented, the land of song, the dragon, the daffodil and the leek sped by. And then Dad told us more about the war and how he was *Off to fight Hitler!*

This presented a different picture in our minds than the one intended. After all, my brothers and my sparse knowledge of warfare was gleaned from playing exciting games of war, enacted with a grey cardboard fort and red-coated lead soldiers who could be shot and resurrected over and over again. A far cry from reality. Terry's eyebrows shot up to join an escaped strand of Amami-flattened hair, and he let out a heartfelt *Cor!* To lighten the mood, Mum told us more about where we were to live:

Until the war is over. With my first cousin, your Aunt Sal, Sarah, on a mountain. Mountain Hare!

Plenty of food for thought there! I had already seen photographs of the snow-topped Swiss mountains in Grandma Rose's encyclopedias. More worrying I had also seen drawings and paintings of the Welsh dragon, and as we neared Merthyr Tydfil, our destination, I had more than Adolf Hitler and the war to be mindful of! For the latter part of our journey, I was on the look out for lambs and the '*Coal black, sloe black mines'* of Dylan's writings (unknown then) and was to see a few later on. The porters said *Dore da* when we arrived at Merthyr station, and I felt a small thrill of understanding, quickly replaced by fear on our white-knuckled ascent up an Everest steep hill – Twynrodyn - in a single decker bus to Mountain Hare. Mum (hastily dabbing 'Evening In Paris' perfume behind her ears and replenishing her lipstick), became more animated as she recognised places she hadn't seen in many years.

There's Jones the bakers, children. Luscious custard slices they make! And that's where your aunt Edna's sister lives.

She pointed a finger. (Edna was her best friend who moved to London before her.) My heart was surely in my mouth, as I clutched the bar of the seat in front as the driver changed gear and the bus shuddered, pausing momentarily, and threatened to send us plummeting down from whence we came.

We arrived safely at the summit as night was dimming dusk and the yellow gorse bushes hugging the hillsides. As if alerted by a psychic bell (or did they hear the bus!) the inhabitants of No. 5, Bryn Terrace - the narrow house clinging (carefully I thought) to the side of the mountain - spilled out over the doorstep to greet us. Self-consciously, we greeted genial Aunt Sal, equally genial husband Uncle Bryn, his mother, a tiny, severe, woefully pale-looking, lady – clothed like a rook (albeit a smiling one) - 'Gran Jones' and gangly, grinning Will John, Aunt Sal's teenaged only son. All were warm and friendly, although I felt a frisson of uncertainty about 'Gran Jones.' Lots of *Lovely*'s filled the cosy room, and after our long, unique journey, we were relieved to have such a welcome. Bryan was roused from sleep on Dad's shoulder, and we were almost royally fed and watered. I was left wondering at the popping gas mantles and drawn to the blazing fire inducing the brass plaque inscribed with the Lord's Prayer in Welsh, on a wall, to dance magically with leaping, golden reflections. It was as if invisible arms embraced us in a warm hug. At home we had less romantic electricity and all mod cons. Another, surprising discovery, was yet one more tenant of our temporary home. She was silent but wagged her tail like a metronome, and was a black and tan bitch called

Marina. Never having had a dog, her presence was appealing.

While the novelty of carrying a candle to bed delighted me, we children were so tired after all the excitement we could hardly climb the stairs. What a day! (Some 200 unofficial evacuees settled – a few temporarily - in Merthyr Tydfil and surrounding towns and villages in the first weeks of the war.) I was soon to realise that not all of Merthyr's children fared as well as we, for in 1939 there were 7,000 unemployed people in the borough, many on the poverty line.

Not having enough to eat was soon brought home to me in a quite dramatic fashion. I befriended a girl my age called Barbara and called on her one day. It was as if I had stepped into a Hans Andersen fairy story of the most dismal kind. Her guardians were two kind, while aged aunts, black-clad and thin: one with a prominent growth in her neck. They bade me sit down while their niece ate her dinner - a bowl of thin broth, laced with a single carrot and a turnip. That was it? No dessert, no bowl of fruit on the table…I gazed around the room. It was flag-stoned with a rag mat at the door and the furniture was minimalist long, long before such a thing was fashionable, plain and scrubbed clean. It was my first experience of real poverty and affected me quite deeply, which highlights how important food has always been to me. Barbara owned no toys that I knew of, except for a spinning top. We played a game that we called 'Dibs' (proper name 'Fivestones') in the dirt yard. Dibs was a game whereby one had to throw a stone in the air and pick up all four on the ground, one by one. I never managed it.

Backtracking, I awoke on that first morning, slightly alarmed not to find 'The House that Jack Built' characters parading around the bedroom border, and was further confused to hear a cockerel crowing? And then the penny dropped. I was in Wales living on the side of a mountain. Helping Bryan dress (Terry refusing to budge) we were lured downstairs like Bisto kids by the magnetic smell of frying bacon, where we found Dad and Uncle Bryn discussing worthy problems, including the war of course, with all due seriousness, while I – after indulging in the tempting fried breakfast – had better things to do. Exploring my new home and surroundings, I discovered that 5 Bryn Terrace's 'best' room: the 'lounge', at the front of the house, looked immaculate and untouched. I later learned it was only used for formal, 'stiffer' occasions – like the laying in state of bodies, fortunately rare –or when the preacher, or someone special, called for tea. Its display cabinet showed off the best china and ornaments; a chaise longue and chairs were over-upholstered. It smelled clean, unloved and a little forbidding. The 'middle' room had a slightly worn strip of carpet advertising it main use; and boasted a treadle sewing machine, much used by Aunt Sal, and was dust-free, polished and very tidy. The dining/living room was the hub of the house, cosy, aromatic, simply furnished and welcoming. Its simple, metal-latched door (which often rattled in the winter winds) led to a narrow yard, built into the side of the mountain, so one had to climb steep steps to reach the chickens living there and the 'dump' which made my eyes gleam. Playing at'house' was a favourite game. The only downside that I could spot was the outside 'lav'with its scrubbed wooden seat and pieces of neatly torn newspaper on a hook. I didn't fancy wiping my bottom on the 'Merthyr Express' newsprint! Even worse, later, was digging through the drifts of snow that gathered in the dip to reach the loo. But, oh the space; the freedom I was already feeling at living on a mountain surrounded by other mountains (in reality grey, coal slag tips, and a few grassy hills and mounds). It was as well that awareness of a serious issue like separation was temporarily absent, replaced by an odd, bubbly, but good feeling in my tummy. The next day, in between shopping, Mum and Dad had their photograph taken down town, their sad images needing no caption. Sharp-eared, I overheard Dad whisper to Mum:

I'll carry it in my breast pocket, Lila, next to my heart, whatever happens.

Too soon, September the 12th dawned and there was a tearful farewell. Dad left, destination unknown, most probably France, where part of his squadron had already been posted. Everyone was subdued, particularly Mum and Terry.

BLACKBERRYING

Brother Terry, aged five, and shy
looked at the world with a wary eye.
And when Dad went away on that war-torn day,
found it difficult not to cry.

Aunt Sal soon warmed to his waifish looks
and took him under her wing:
"There's a nuisance this ol' war is!"
her voice it seemed to sing.

But however hard she cajoled and pleaded,
his mood remained so sad and
pale as uncooked pastry, he repeated
"I just want my Dad!"

Mum and I joined in the pleas –
all to no avail;
he was like Tiny Tim without a crutch –
and quite beyond the pale.

Soon after that the sun came out
and Aunt Sal had a thought…
"Why don' you two go blackberry pickin'!
I really think you ought."

And so, armed with enamel jugs
we clambered up over the hills
filled with thoughts of luscious fruit -

Aunt Sal had found an antidote for brother Terry's ills.

Despite missing Dad and seeing Mum sad, we children soon found that living amid such space on a virtually traffic free road when compared to our busy one in Dagenham, was an absolute joy. Previously, even the shortest journeys or trips, without adult supervision, were taboo. The large area of grassland and scrub behind Aunt Sal's house contained, not only clucking chickens and a few sheds, but a communal dump on which were thrown such desirable items as old curtains, bits of lino, ancient mats, broken 'po's, corrugated iron (*Wow!*) bricks and handleless crockery. Ingredients for building and furnishing houses aplenty. The nearest I had ever got to making even a den, was either in our back garden, or in a bushy field behind Grandma Rose's house where an old lace curtain over a hollowed out bush and a doll's tea-set sufficed. (I was always and still am fascinated by architecture and house interiors. Had I been blessed with a superior grip of maths - I am a duffer in that direction - I might have ended up as an architect or designer. Playful thought.)

And so, with Mum still at our sides, we explored our new surroundings before being reluctantly introduced to our new school which stood just behind the giddyingly steep Twynrodyn hill. We were in no rush to enrol sooner than was necessary. It wasn't long (it never was) before news of our arrival had spread around our small community. Relatives, friends and neighbours popped in to greet us. Blodwen

-'the voice' in my memory: a lively, 'fun' lady - who lived a few doors up was first, then our immediate neighbour Mrs Bevan, face arranged in greeting mode, said: *Call me Auntie Cassie,* followed by Mrs Davies and her fair-haired daughter Joan, about my age, I thought. Hard on their heels were aunt Mary Ellen, Aunt Sal's kind sister who lived in Merthyr town, with her husband, shy uncle Tom, a miner. When we called in to see Uncle Tom at a later date, he was as black as night (the first time we had sight of a miner) and after his bath in the tin tub by the fire in the kitchen, we didn't recognize him and thought him a lodger, which he found very funny. Yet another cousin, Aunt Nelen, lived with her husband and only son, Islwyn, in a desirable, detached cottage, surrounded by lush foliage. When visiting her later, she pointed out the dock leaves: *'Andy if you should get caught short, love*...she told me with a guffaw. Giant rhubarb bushes and a multitude of flowers also grew in her semi-wild plot, a little further up the mountain. We were overwhelmed!

Also exciting, was the prospect of being taught to tap dance by cousin Islwyn, who could not only dance a mean Time-Step, but also owned a pleasing baritone voice, along with his Dad, whose voice seemed to come from the very bowels of the earth. We were also introduced to a prefabricated 'Community Centre' situated nearby, where concerts and plays were performed, and which proved to be a sanity saver for the many women on the mountain, most of their men-folk being either down the mines or in the armed forces. Islwyn and his Dad were already rehearsing for an imminent show *"The Wreck of the Argosy"* and there was talk of putting on another show where children were needed to sing and dance. Now my singing could only be compared to caterwauling, although Mum foolishly encouraged it. I was painfully aware that if I opened my lungs and let rip, I could clear a room in two minutes flat. Dancing was different. I had inherited a natural rhythm from Mum and Grandad Sam (both nimble on their feet and the winners of many prizes for ballroom dancing) and was learning more steps each day. I was in my element, while slightly concerned as the colour heightened in my cheeks and someone or something was racing around my heart, that I had a fever coming on!

LIZZIE THE BOGIE

MUCH LIKE THE BLAND, single story chapel bang next door to Aunt Sal's house, "Lizzie the Bogie" was an 'unknown quantity,' and a slightly unsettling one at that. A bogie was something unpleasant and dirty that inhabited your nose – which you removed when no one was looking - or had the word 'man' attached to it, which invited sweaty palms and made you look about you. Wasn't it? I had heard her mentioned since my arrival on Mountain Hare, for she was a local character with a reputation but I hadn't met her and only knew that *She tells fortunes*

As my brother Terry and I nervously entered the temporarily sun-warmed whilst uninviting chapel next to our present home (urged by the grown-ups and mindful that, if we didn't, God could peep in the windows of No. 5 and seek us out for punishment) on that very first Sunday, a girl with fair to brown hair, about my height, sidled up close to me, in conspiratorial manner.

Lizzie the Bogie tol' our Mam that she'll 'ave another baby soon! she whispered.

How does she know? I asked, puzzled. At seven, my knowledge of the reproduction process was of the stork and gooseberry bush variety.

Well, she sorta knows everythin' – like God – she lives up the Bogie road

(It took me a while to mentally translate this statement into common sense, at first toying with the idea that God did indeed live up the Bogie road in Lizzie's house, an intriguing possibility.) Strangers until then, the little girl and I chatted on like old friends. Was it Susie or Joyce Rogers?

I've heard people mention Lizzie the Bogie but WHO is she? Is she like a witch? I asked her.

Oh no, mun. She isn't a witch. Fancy you've not met 'er!

Well, I only came to live here a week ago.

Oh! So you're that Lunduner they're all talkin' about. I thought you talked posh like.

I don't talk posh! I said, indignantly.

And I don't come from London. I come from Dagenham in Essex. Who's talking about me? I could feel my cheeks growing redder. Being an object of curiosity was new to me. She shrugged. *Everybody!* She said. I suddenly didn't feel like the *Nonentity* Dad called me when I made him cross. Being an evacuee and a bit important held a new appeal. I suddenly bucked up a bit. It was a rather nice feeling.

Terry stuck close to me, limpet-like. Despite the boost to my ego as we entered the cooler interior of the chapel, I was nervous This was unknown territory. I held his hand and tried reassuring him, while needing reassurance myself!.

You still haven't told me much about Lizzie the Bogie, I said to my new friend, my curiosity stoked.

Well, she tends geese and tells fortunes. Even rich people from all over comes an' gets 'er to read their palms and the tea leaves. Some sez they gives 'er LOTS of money. But she still goes around without any shoes on, so I don' know so much...

I was fascinated. We didn't have anyone

remotely like Lizzie the Bogie in Dagenham that I knew of, apart from an odd woman in nearby Dagenham-Heathway who used to make up her face like a painted doll and scrub out dustbins. I later learned that quite prominent people preferred to seek Lizzie's advice and glimpse into the future rather than trust more professional fortune tellers, so she must have had a gift of sorts. As time passed, I heard that Lizzie had a son called Dai (as common a name as confetti at a wedding). Our Mum also had a cousin Dai and the two were friends. One story doing the rounds was that Lizzie heard the two Dais plotting to have a dip in a nearby pond.

You be careful, my boy, she said. ...*come back year drowned, and I'll bloody well kill you!*

Dai one (Mum's cousin) recalled being invited to tea: she was very hospitable.

Sit you down, she'd say....*if you wan' a cake, 'ave two.*

But back to that first Sunday and the visit to the chapel. My new friend and I continued to chatter in whispers. *'Ush now!* A vinegary, elderly lady in bombazine black, put a finger to her lips.Terry, pale and mute, shrank in his clothes and slumped down in his bench seat so that he was hardly there at all, while I swallowed extra hard and tried to sit up straight as Mum was always telling me to. We didn't utter another word, until prompted to sing hymns. Mr Evans, that week's Speaker, peered over his glasses and gave us a half-smile before warning all and sundry about the:

Evils of the flesh and the *Terrible punishment which awaits us all if we stray from the path.*

I was clueless on both counts, except for maybe telling the odd fib or two to save my bacon. *It wasn't ME that ate that last piece of chocolate!*

Fortunately, Grandad Havard (a fair warbler) had taught us part of 'Calon Lan', although most of the hymns merged and sounded like double Dutch while us two novices opened and closed our mouths now and then pretending we were anything but. It's strange that I don't remember ever meeting Lizzie the Bogie, but I surely must have? I have discovered that memory is very selective, sometimes unreliable and occasionally suggests we are liars. I mostly salvage what floats to the surface, though now and then I coax stubborn events from dark corners (like winkles with pins) and they can be surprisingly compliant and crystal clear as if they happened yesterday, or maybe the day before. But back to Mountain Hare…Oh, what a different, strange new world I had been thrust into by the actions of a man whose face and stature I was only familiar with via newsreels, but of whose evilness I was made well aware. He had, after all, taken our Dad away from us and sent him to a foreign country, many miles away, which made us and our Mum very sad. Mummy said that we should: *Pray for the poor children in Poland,* which we did. I added a P.S. *Please send Dad back and end the war.*

I was beginning to learn that not all prayers are answered. Dad didn't return then, and the war continued. It crossed my mind that maybe God hadn't heard and was with Lizzie the Bogie having his fortune told, or maybe just having two cakes with his tea.

MERTHYR AND ME AT WAR

NATURALLY WITH US CHILDREN being so young, we were ignorant, in the main, of the allied war's progress or otherwise. The only way Terry and I could help the war effort, in a very meagre way of course, was by collecting waste paper, and I doubt that it amounted to much! However during the following year, I was delighted to be able to dance in concerts where the takings were given to various groups to help the troops abroad. Not that I was a leading light. Far from it. But being quite small for my age, I was usually the 'baby' of the older group, which sometimes worked in my favour.

How different it was for the grown-ups! Whether or not they were employed before the outbreak of war, and whatever their vocation or way of life, they were suddenly plunged into a totally different world. Most of the able-bodied men – if not mining for coal or exempt for others reasons - found themselves in strange uniforms and often in strange countries. And whilst we were ignorant of the worst that war can bring, we were very aware that our Dad and his youngest brother Bernard wore Air Force blue; Dad busy (later) as a "plane movement plotter" and Uncle Bernard as an airborne navigator.

As has been written about elsewhere, Merthyr Tydfil played host to many mothers and children during the first part of the war; our family being among the first to arrive. However, several evacuees left to be settled elsewhere and some even returned to London, preferring to risk danger rather than live with strangers, however kind. In London itself, the main-line stations continued their roles as mute witnesses to pathetic scenes as some half a million women and their mostly bewildered offspring left for various destinations.

To us children, Hitler had, hitherto, been a name that crackled over the wireless waves or appeared in newsprint. However, as his ranting and raving became more familiar to us, via newsreels at the cinema, his evil image took on comic overtones. No one could be that fanatical, that evil, could they? With us being innocent and more or less uncomprehending, he became a figure of fun to imitate and ridicule with strutting goose steps and enthusiastic 'Sieg Heils'. There was strong competition in the school playground as to who did the best Hitler!

Due to the very nature of war, things naturally changed. Food hoarding was warned against. This was particularly ironic, for many had just about enough for the next meal, and many didn't! There was also a request for blankets. However, there was not an abundance of anything worth talking about for the masses in Merthyr then. In downtown Merthyr, bland, serious and fixed-smiling faces atop grey pinstripe and Harris tweed suits with price tags of two pounds ten shillings and three pounds, stared unseeing out of Burton's window at a stream of humanity passing by with a new, urgent tempo in its step. The town had become a hub of activity, with an endless supply of sandbags to fill and queues of volunteers signing up for military service. Eventually, earlier confusion gave way to sanity as ARP wardens and evacuation committees did their best. The war was, at last, to provide work for the many thousands long idle through no fault of their own. Irony was the word of the times.

Our community, set apart and elevated as it was, looked down on the bustling town with a sleepy eye. In between brief respites, rumours of enemy attacks and infiltration continued to spread in epidemic proportions. There were plenty of willing tongues around! The local newspaper again urged people to keep calm, underlining the need to zip our lips. *Careless Talk Costs Lives* appeared emblazoned on posters.

It's as well you knows no National Secrets young lady!

Aunt Sal said to me with a grin, for I was a bit of a chatterbox at times. Of course most of the really serious talk of war skimmed over our heads. I was reminded years later of the sinking of the "Athenia" by a German submarine; and the more urgent appeals for mobilisation continued. Before the end of September, it was said that 500 lives had been lost when the "Courageous," a British aircraft carrier, was sunk, but I only recall talk of a Merthyr boy surviving the sinking and being much feted on his return home. Five hundred deaths was too staggering a figure for the young to digest. An unexpected trip to Cardiff (Aunt Sal's brother Uncle Jim ran '*The Canadian*' public house there, complete with fascinating dumb waiter and bowling alley) delighted us. A snapshot of the time shows us with Dad – so he must have had extra leave after returning from France at a later date. Details are lost but I recall silvery barrage balloons like surreal elephants: a whole herd of them, hoveringly ungainly over Cardiff docks. Brother Terry was particularly intrigued. We were to see them in a multitude of places before the war's end and soon accepted them as part of the sky's new novel décor.

Doubtless, most adults were alert and anxious, hardly knowing what to expect on any one day, but fortunately, the anticipated holocaust did not materialise when war was first declared, not in Great Britain or France at least. The armies faced each other on the French border early in that freezing icy winter of 1939, but scarcely a gun was fired.

It was, of course, a far different story for many thousands of the poor Polish people, especially those of the Jewish race. However, it was several years before the whole horrific truth of German fanaticism was known.

When rationing was put into effect, I at first hated that rubbery, reconstituted mess known as scrambled eggs, but after a while got used to it, along with many other 'inconveniences.' However, at least Aunt Sal's few chickens saw that we had a few extra fresh eggs from time to time. She and Mum were dab hands at making a little go a long way and poems should have been written about their dumpling and vegetable soups and stews, their aromatic bread puddings, plus bread and 'marge' fruit puddings (no shortage of milk or cream that I recall) as well as Teisan Lap -Welsh cake- and Welsh griddle cakes, heavy with fruit (was Mum fluttering her eyelashes again!) Apples too seemed to be plentiful, and blackberries and whinberries of course, when in

49

season. Fortunately, in our house, hunger was a stranger.

One eerie effect of being at war was being out on moonless nights – usually with an adult - when the blackout was enforced. Houses and other buildings were dark, threatening outlines: silhouettes (with black/navy curtains at the windows, masking the lights inside). Most of us had torches – with strict instructions to never: *I repeat NEVER,* warned Uncle Bryn, shine them upwards and only switch them on when absolutely necessary. There were several reports in the newspaper of people being injured and some killed by cars during those innumerable, seemingly never ending, dark nights. It was safer when the moon didn't shine over all (from the point of view of the enemy attacking us), but there always seemed a price to pay!

Cousin Will John had a fair haired, pretty girlfriend, Janet, whom he later married, and one night – just before he signed up to join the Air Force – he, she and a few friends went out for a drink or three. Returning quite late, nearing Mountain Hare, they spied something white in a nearby field and stood stock still, fearful that a German airman had parachuted from a plane. With fingers on lips, they quietly gathered a few sticks to arm themselves and stealthily approached the field, protected by dense foliage. Apparently, there was a stile, over which they climbed and then ran into the field whooping and brandishing their weapons. They said afterwards that they didn't know who was the most surprised – them or the lone white horse, trying to take a nap under a tree! (Shades of 'Dad's Army.')

One distraction from 'war talk' was regularly attending Sunday school, and often – of an evening – 'Seion' the old chapel situated on Twynrodyn Hill. It was a very popular place then and people had always flocked there in droves to listen to 'The Word' from places as far apart as Aberdare and Cwmnedd in the Neath Valley. However, because of the war, there were far more women, children and elderly men attending then. An inscription outside the building always saddened me as it was 'Sacred to the memory of the eighteen children of John and Mary Treharne, all of whom died in infancy.' I couldn't even begin to imagine their shared grief. The Seion building dated back to the 1700s and boasted a splendid pipe organ; the acoustics being such that, with the exception of yours truly, everyone, or so it seemed, sounded like angels! The Welsh are surely blessed when it comes to singing. Even so, I cannot now think that I sat so long without fidgeting or longing to be elsewhere!

SEION

Rev. Davies (first name David)
as tall a man as I had seen –
cleared his throat, and eyebrows mating,
let his dark eyes sweep the scene.

All within that chilly chapel
sat up straight and neat and trim –
some composed others fearful,
masking turmoil deep within.

51

He sternly spoke of theft and greed
and coveting another's bride;
spoke of hope and charity
and the sin of too much pride.

The Rev. Davies scanned the pews –
looking for (I surmised)
sinners who had strayed, were lost,
revealing guilt in troubled eyes.

I recalled a fib I'd told
and trembled through and through,
as Rev Davies ranted on and promised,
pointing…"If you've sinned, the only price is
 HELL FOR YOU!"

His finger bore into my soul
and I vowed there on that Sunday,
never again to tell a fib –
and didn't 'til the Monday.

THE WHITE TIP AND THE FUNERAL

IT WASN'T LONG BEFORE I discovered that life in a Welsh community was a far cry from that experienced by a sheltered existence in Dagenham. For starters, the White Tip (think grey) near Mountain Hare was haunted. Or so it was said…And with a wild imagination shaping up nicely as artist, and a desolate landscape as canvas, it was easy enough to believe. On one particular journey, ominous coal slag-tips loomed, as threatening as bogeymen at night, to merge with a darkening, unpromising sky. An afternoon in evening's overcoat! Factually, a steamroller crashed down over the edge of the White Tip many years before and the two men and a dog, unfortunately in its path, were, *Squashed flat!* Mum told us, perhaps a little too dramatically (she'd have made a good actress!). I was, naturally, shocked and wide-eyed but could thank 'Desperate Dan' for diluting the gruesome scene, for it was a known fact that enlarged, pancake flat victims of steamrollers could be rolled up, scraped up, or indeed could get up of their own accord. Couldn't they? However, a few of the local children - especially the older ones - liked promoting the story and suggested that:

Their poor, restless, spirits wander abroad whenever they have a fancy, or so it is said! Thereby raising the story to another level. But having first planted the seed, Mum, aware of her foolishness, said *It's a load of rubbish. There's no such things as ghosts!* My belief was on a see-saw. First the inferno, then the cup of water…I always passed the White Tip

in haste. Nevertheless, footloose and fancy free –
having wondered what Mum's birthplace: Pwyllywiad
(or in English, Duckspool) further on up the mountain
looked like - I plodded on, with Joan Davies in tow. A
shortish, uphill, walk away from Bryn Terrace, feet
and mind not quite in accord, but with spiralling smoke
beckoning in the distance, I headed towards it, my
interest gradually growing with each step. Curiosity
became master of the moment. Disappointingly, I
found that there wasn't much to explore, after all.
There were ducks and a large puddle masquerading as
a pool – it had apparently shrunk over the years – but I
had expected more. A huddle of cottages – four in all -
squatted near a meagre helping of greenery – mostly
blackberried, elderberry bushes, brown edged ferns,
and a few windblown and straggly dog roses threaded
through the hedgerows, all overlooked by the familiar,
dark slag mounds. The sombre scene was further
brightened a little by a few patches of yellowing grass,
and clumps of dandelions and dock leaves, but I soon
saw that the venue of Mum's birth was a dreary dot of
a place. No roses around that doorway! The cottages
(needing a lot of TLC) consisted of two rooms up and
two down; had no front gardens and scant back yards.
Some were still flag-stoned inside, with rag mats at the
front and back doors.

*When it rained heavy, we could sweep the
blackened sludge through from back to front, or the
other way around!* Grandma Sal had told us. Ugh! I
couldn't then visualise my Grandad Sam proudly
carrying his new wife, Sarah Jane, over the threshold
of their modest cottage on the day they were married in

1905, or the good, bad and hard times they would experience within its walls. They would both talk of this later, when pressed. There wasn't much else to take in, however. Was it then, or another time that I noticed the watercress growing in the ditches, and the large birds flying overhead – vultures? In reality carrion crow. I rarely ventured further - across the often wind/rain- swept terrain – where Dowlais (venue of my grandparents' former greengrocers/general shop) lay, without a playmate to accompany me – usually Joan Davies or Joyce Rogers, for it could be an off-putting, bleak landscape in winter and could whip any bare flesh into a sore and reddened state in no time. Gloves and long socks were a must; Vaseline a boon. My mind's eye reveals a large, elaborate tomb, enclosed by cruel, dagger tipped railings in the area, and a mini dust-storm – like an image from a Western film – which surely must have inhabited a nightmare rather than a dream? Someone mentioned the "Hound of the Baskervilles" – I was familiar with the story – and certain scenes are inexorably linked. (Returning many years later, several times, I never did locate the tomb.) Did I look in the wrong place? Did it feature in a nightmare, after all?

Another source of fear were geese. With their outstretched necks, loud squawking, and speedy gait, I skirted them with a wary eye. During one lone exploration (braver than usual) I disturbed one from a flock - the devil fowlified? - near Mum's old home, and it chased me further and closer than usual so that I, dry-mouthed, panicked, fell over and grazed a knee. Hobbling home, dabbing the dripping blood at intervals with a hankie from within my navy knickers, I arrived at 5 Bryn Terrace to tell Aunt Sal of the geese (note the plural) which ferociously attacked me. Had I already observed that a little drama always solicited more concern? Of course, she tutted, did a lot of *Dew, dewing*...tended to my scratch and made me a calming cup of tea, before placing me before a roaring fire to recuperate. Studying the delicate and vibrant colours in the flames always mesmerised me. What flights of fancy it brought forth! Vivid orange fairies danced and fanned themselves with electric blue fans; forests and castles burned.

Two other events are linked in my head. The death of a teenaged male friend, Royston's, aged grandfather – who, Royston told us in vivid fashion and detail,

Suddenly appeared, mun – at the foot of my bed – all floaty and ghost-like, the night after 'e died. I never seen a ghost before, but it musta been my grandad. 'anging like in the air 'e was...

Whether Royston did indeed see a ghost or not was open to question, but the way he told of it put the fear of God into all members of his young audience. The other event was witnessing my first Welsh funeral. Whether they were actually linked cannot be verified. However, I can recall what put me in mind of black clad 'penguin men' (no women) – slowly waddling/marching, singing at full throttle, in a long line on a freezing, snowy day, behind a silk flower bedecked hearse, bearing the deceased to the cemetery. I wrote the following poem many years later as the incident remained a firm cameo.

FUNERAL OF 1940

My eyes grew wide with wonder,
my ears grew wider still,
as the voices of those penguin men
drifted up over the hill.

"Royston's grandad's passed away"
 a childish voice did say
"There's sad," another voice opined
on that bitter, winter's day.

Dylan's 'bible-black' they wore,
boots were sloe-black too;
unlike the black be-ribboned hearse
with flowers of every hue.

Later in the 'Gluepot' –
happier than sad …
they drank to Royston's granddad –
"Nearly ninety! E didn't do bad."
"Shame they couldn't bury 'im –
God rest 'is poor ol' soul –
the ground was much too frozen
to dig the bloody 'ole!" .

*****

It was said in Wales that, no matter what you had or
hadn't achieved on earth, when you died you acquired
a special status! I thought it a shame that the corpse

couldn't know that.

A VICTIM OF FASHION

MOST LITTLE GIRLS OF seven and eight, if they are feminine types, enjoy dressing up, and I - whilst giving in to occasional tomboy leanings – was no exception.

However, in the nineteen thirties and forties, the majority of children weren't indulged, unless very spoilt or rich, as to what they had to wear. Being fashionable then, and often a stark necessity for working-class women, a predominance of the larger group sewed and knitted, so their offspring quite naturally accepted whatever was fashioned for them. Children rarely had any choice in the matter. (Unlike now!) Style had little to do with it. Looking back, I was extraordinarily fortunate in that I had two paternal aunts – one my Godmother (Doris) – whose fingers could work magic and whose taste bordered on mine. They also belonged to the "well heeled" side of the family; certainly not my financially depleted maternal, Welsh side. Exciting parcels arrived at No.5 Bryn Terrace every now and then stuffed with sweaters, berets, scarves and socks, and occasionally, knitted two pieces and appliquéd skirts and dresses, all beautifully made and desirable.

My two aunts' fingers were rarely still. The younger, Doris, was fair haired, pretty, and runner up to Southend's Beauty Queen one year. Their annual Carnival was a grand pageant in the thirties. The older sister, Eileen (Girlie), had what were called 'lucky gaped teeth' and was also an inspired pianist. Her hauntingly beautiful rendition of 'Rustle of Spring' often echoes in my head. Both women were Convent educated. They knitted Fair Isle patterns under the framed gaze of revered Winston Churchill whilst chatting about the Royal family's latest outfits (a favourite subject) or whatever else took their fancy, and they embroidered for their mother - my silvery-haired Grandma Rose – exquisite tablecloths and napkins, et al. They also dressed dolls in gorgeous clothes for charity; and their own underwear had me gasping with admiration. In comparison, I lagged far behind, for aunt Doris made me nervous (being kind but bossy) when I sewed under her eagle eye and my pitiful work would end up grimy with sweat, with stitches too tight and knitting too loose. Sadly, a seamstress/knitter I would never be, although I fashioned some passable cushions, patchwork and collages in later years.

One day, with the war raging elsewhere and peace reigning on "our" mountain, the postman delivered a larger than usual package which had us three children twitching with anticipation. In war torn London, probably spurred on by the boredom of making repetitive khaki uniforms, with no break in sight, Uncle Ben, the tailor – one of Dad's many cousins – took time off to make the three of us children two pairs of long trousers each. The parcelled apparel was received with itchy fingered interest, and on my part in particular, some puzzlement as we examined the contents. I mean, LONG TROUSERS! For a girl? Absolutely unheard of then. Whatever was he thinking! Even my brothers were surprised for, in those days, only older lads wore their trousers long (so what that the younger ones had frozen knee-caps!).

Terry was five, while Bryan was only three. However, realising how smart and warm they were, they were soon won over. On the other hand, the subject of ME wearing long trousers nearly raised the roof! I too was, at first, incredulous at such a crazy idea – a reaction echoed by the rest of the household, especially by Gran Jones' (narrow as an arrow) quarter. She shook her head and tutted and insinuated that I'd immediately become a sort of mini Jezebel if I wore them. However, with the bitterly cold weather as my best ally, and Mum's persuasiveness working, I reluctantly put on a pair. They were made of bluey-green tweed wool, and although they itched a bit, I had to admit that they were snug and warm. But oh, what a mini-storm on a mountain they were about to whip up!!

Fashions were fast changing in London, but on Mountain Hare things were more ponderous and we were a far cry away. On the first morning I wore what was to become a subject of discussion, almost as fascinating as the war itself... I was aware of more than the odd glance and nudge. Did I pose or preen? Maybe. Although I was rather shy. I really can't say. What I can say is that the matter, quite literally, came to a head (mine) a few days later.

Rummaging on "our dump" – a favourite pastime after school – I was searching, with fast numbing fingers, for something to enhance the look of my latest "house" – more of an igloo at the time – built from broken bricks, discarded bits of timber, and battered remnants of corrugated iron sheeting. Concentrating on the job in hand, I was caught completely off guard and knocked for six by a hard projectile.

BULLS EYE! a triumphant voice yelled from the top of a nearby shed as I staggered to my feet. Verbal abuse swiftly followed. (Was it Connie? My memory can't be sure.)

Go back to Lundun, evacuee! We don' wan' you year with your fancy trousers... 'Oo do you think you are?

The enemy was still positioned on the shed roof, her well aimed missile: a broken bottle, having, painfully, found its target. And there was me thinking that all the action was happening abroad! Just then, blood started oozing into my eyes as I became aware of a pain in my cranium. Convinced I wasn't long for this world, I ran in tears to aunt Sal. She gently probed for glass fragments, tutting like mad and saying:

I don' know what children are coming to these days...

Blood dripped copiously into a hastily found bowl, increasing my fears that death was at my elbow. I was further anguished and embarrassed to be relieved of a tidy clump of my hair so that the wound could be properly cleaned and dressed. Luckily, I just missed being hospitalised by Aunt Sal's expert attention. The worst indignity of all though was having to wear a beret until my hair grew back again - to you know whose delight. Ironically, within a month or two, at least half a dozen girls and women were sporting trousers on and around Mountain Hare.

You were just a victim of fashion!

Mum was later heard to say. Hardly much

consolation to a seven year old, whose pride, as well as her person, had been so sorely wounded.

THE COMMUNITY CENTRE

AUNT SAL SAID:

The Centre's breathed new life into Mountain Hare!

And I must say I agreed with her, for it generated a lot of excitement in both adults and children. A plain, prefabricated building set a little to the right of her house on the opposite side of the road looking up Mountain Hare; it was the venue of many activities. The owners – and there were many – of rich voices, rejoiced in their ability to shine. Secretly entrepreneurial types, suddenly found their feet, puffed up their chests and started getting busy, adjusting stage scripts, auditioning would-be actors, prompting, coaching dancers and singers, et al. Of the men left who hadn't yet, or were too mature to join the Forces, many also came forward to assist in the making, painting and moving of scenery sets, as well as the vital 'warblers.' Cousin Islwyn and his Dad, Uncle Tom, were amongst the latter group. Singers, both male and female, from further afield soon got wind of the Centre's plans and were also auditioned. 'The Farmers Arms' (alias 'The Gluepot') nearby was only too happy to aid the cause by lubricating their vocal chords before, and after practice. And, on the heels of the successful *'Wreck of the Argosy,'* to provide celebration drinks all round. In point of fact, the pub did a roaring trade, so the Centre was responsible for not only putting more smiles on more faces, but helped to boost the finances of our local public house.

Whispers reached us that a production of '*The*

Merry Milkmaids' was to begin forthwith and a whole troupe of dancers, singers and actors, was required to audition.

A King and Queen of the Fairies, plus their subjects, were put through their paces (including yours truly) with Nan - a sturdier, older girl cast as King – and pretty, dainty, fair haired Myra as Queen. Excellent casting as an ancient, hand painted, photograph confirms. Being required to prance about and wave wands wasn't too difficult for us amateurs, and dressed in gold satin and tulle with circlets of gold tinsel in our hair, we thought we were the bees knees. Although I could look to no professional thespian heritage that I knew of, I was light on my feet, like Mum, and Grandad before her. It was hardly an arduous role, and as I wasn't required to sing, no one 'headed for the hills…'Treading the boards' was a new and exciting prospect for the future. The stuff of childish dreams.

Came the opening –valiantly suppressing first night nerves –no one threw up and we performed to an enthusiastic audience. Mums, aunts and sundry relatives proved very loyal, and there were even a few '*Bravo's'* (possibly bribed). A photographer from '*The Merthyr Express'* was present. A camera flashed. We were famous! I was hooked….(Nerves set in later!)

There was then a lull in stage productions for a while as people became busy with war work. Thereafter, the women sewed and knitted frenziedly for the troops, and as a relief from their tasks, a Keep Fit class was formed and multi-shaped ladies could be seen, in navy knickers and white tops, leaping around, touching their toes and swinging their arms willy nilly. Having a penchant for the ladies, Uncle Bryn in particular thought the introduction of such a class most interesting and was told (by his mother!) to keep away from the Centre's windows. He couldn't have taken much notice as Mum recalled him commenting:

You should see the size of some of the be'inds in those navy knickers, Lila!

She said that some of the younger lads had as many ganders as they could get away with which caused a few, harmless, guffaws during sessions, not that the ladies themselves appreciated it! Not surprisingly, Gran Jones, thinking that the devil was at work, turned up her nose at such *Goings on...* and, although I didn't always know what she was tutting about, she did a lot of tutting from time to time. Being quite deaf, she was suspicious that she was being talked about (which she sometimes was). She was not a tolerant lady and adhered to no make up and no nonsense, her pleasures bound up in singing hymns and attending chapel. However, it must be said, she did have a warm heart as it was her suggestion that we be 'taken in' while the war reigned, for she was the owner of No.5, Bryn Terrace. Sadly, her patience didn't always extend to her daughter- in-law, Aunt Sal, who came from a rare mould, for she would remind her that she was 'Queen Bee' and legal owner of the house. I cannot recall the slights she inflicted on poor Aunt Sal, but Mum told me that she *Led her a hard life, and was a bit of a Tartar!* I was a great fan of Aunt Sal. She was ace in my eyes. Equipped with enviable tolerance and kindness, she had the capacity to be happy and make the most of almost any situation. In the early years of her marriage to Uncle Bryn, she suffered the grief of having three stillborn daughters, and although her only son, Will John, survived, his twin - a girl- also died. Due to complications at the birth, she was left with a badly ulcerated leg, which was treated but never healed during her long life. She suffered much pain stoically, walked countless miles, worked the treadle sewing machine for hours on end, kept the house spotless - and more noticeable to me than her other good traits then was a dab hand at cooking.

Oh, Aunt Sal! I would exclaim, round-eyed and appreciative, as she produced yet another batch of delicious Welsh cakes. As well as gymnastics, the group attending the Centre was shown how to stitch leather and make wallets, purses and handbags; also how to make flowers out of old stockings and fine wire, and colourful, woolen pom-poms to sew onto hats and sweaters. When it rained, although a bit heavy handed at first, I soon learned and enjoyed helping with the latter. Although discovered, television was only present in the homes of the wealthy, but was destined to change people's lives - some more than others - and make a huge hole in the arts and crafts movement for a while!

Apart from the above, there were many social gatherings in the Centre, which provided solace for the ladies left behind and missing their men folk in the Forces. Mum regularly thumped out such numbers as: *'Roll out the Barrel,' 'South of the Border,'' 'Ang out your Washing on the Siegfried Line,'* and *'Amapola'* on the piano - all sang to with much gusto, and real morale boosters. I, fortunately, refrained from joining in. I can only recall one more show there in which I took part. More little hearts aflutter - dressed to kill in a ghastly 'shitty yellow' satin outfit, red gauntlets sprinkled with glitter – almost garrotted by the tight elastic-strapped, pill box hat and daubed with vermillion lipstick, I was required to perform a military dance and sing two songs : '*Kith me Goodnight Thergeant Major*' and '*The Quartermarthterth Thtores*' as two front teeth were missing at the time. Nobody seemed to mind much, although there were a few giggles I didn't have the heart to interpret! A feeling of euphoria remained long after the greasepaint had been removed, and then one day Mum said, wearing a broad smile,

I've heard of a good dancing teacher called Patricia Lewis who has a studio in down- town Merthyr. Would you like lessons?

Would I?!! What I didn't then know, was that Mum's deferred decision to do war work was imminent and the lessons were planned as a distraction. Mum had, after all, always been the pivot of my existence for over seven years. Oh how I would miss her and her cuddles!

POWELL THE GROCER, OTHER NEIGHBOURS AND THE MARKET

AS THE BOTTLE THROWING incident became a dim, while painful, memory, I was gradually accepted by the 'enemy' as a friendly contemporary rather than an alien evacuee. It was as well for, at seven, I didn't like being out of step with anyone. Oh boy no! I overheard Aunt Sal saying:

The children are amazingly resilient, whatever that meant, and soon became used to a slightly different routine and way of life. Horizons were vast, fences less encroaching; the sun more watery, the air fresher: some-times downright cold, but there was much to be enjoyed. And oh that space around! Whilst some faces lose their features over time and distance, kindness and interest can more easily be recalled. Two people I have mentioned before: our pleasant neighbour, 'Aunt Cassie,' and further down our terrace the very lively, humorous lady, undoubtedly Queen of the local characters, Mrs Steadman. Her fame had preceded her presence. In fair weather and foul, she wore a small felt or knitted hat pulled down over her grey curls. When fine, she sat on her front step for a gossip with anyone who had the time and inclination.

Come to the 'alf a crown side, now, she'd say, pointing to her 'good' ear. If rain or snow threatened it was:

Inside for Welsh cakes and tea, eh!

There were many who said *Butter wooden melt in 'er mouth? There's a joke!*

The truth was, Mrs Steadman – despite her

69

little lady lost look – could tell a gutsy joke or six and make no mistake. Of course, I heard her laughter and she joked with me, but her earthier 'gems' were reserved for the grown-ups. Prescribed glasses in her eighties, she thought them *A bloody nuisance,* hardly wore them, sat on a few pair and continued to peer at everyone through half closed eyes. At the Queen's Silver Jubilee celebrations, dressed to kill, she was chosen as 'Queen' for the day and much feted. How she lapped up all the attention! She lived until she was 96 and was sorely missed by the community when she died.

Another woman, introduced to me by Uncle Bryn as: *Miss Pritchard: A real lady* occupied a modest cottage, set in an equally modest orchard (garden?) further down the hill. There she lived, all her life apparently, a 'spinster woman' keeping house for her two bachelor brothers. I enjoyed occasionally visiting the trio and the aromas of that time and place are with me still. The bitter sweet and earthy smell of apples from the tree by the front door, and sometimes the aroma of a stew bubbling away on the black-leaded stove. Plus the even more pervading smell of pipe tobacco and spent matches, for the men – it seemed – always had a pipe clenched between their teeth. The Pritchard brothers, usually on the quiet side, were full of bonhomie to me, offering me a penny or an apple to dance the 'Time Step' or the 'Hornpipe', and I'd sometimes blush and shyly oblige. I enjoyed 'pleasing' it seemed.

It's easy to recognise Mr. Powell the grocer in my mental rerun…there he is in his usual beige linen overall like a benign uncle, dispensing sugar in blue paper bags, or whatever else his customers required. You never quite knew what half a pound of broken biscuits would consist of! Would there be iced gems, or chocolate fingers (favourites)? More likely plain digestives or 'Nice' biscuits with maybe a special one thrown in now and then. Mr Powell must have been an agreeable man as I can never recall him being rude or angry and he always had time to chat. I seemed to like 'chatting...' Once a week, Terry and I were allowed to buy a small cache of sweets and chocolates (never too many after rationing of course) and it was fun weighing up dolly mixtures or fruit gums on my toy shop scales and popping them in tiny bags for my 'customers.'

Like most children, I seemed to have an eager appetite for change and new experiences and my first visit to Merthyr market was a memorable one. The most outstanding – nose-wise – were the faggots and peas, their hunger-evoking smell wafting tauntingly on the cold air. Then came the sweet stall with hell-hot, V for victory lozenges, tooth-hurtingly sweet, pink and white coconut ice, and large aniseed balls which you removed from your mouth periodically to inspect their diminishing size. Naturally, the toy stall also appealed. I so enjoyed watching the coloured, metallic acrobats working their magic: walking across tightropes and climbing ladders, etc., and the tiny 'chickens' pecking their feed from boards when you pulled a cord. Also eye- catching, were the celluloid dolls with garish feathers stuck in headbands and around their waists. But more desirable was a kaleidoscope, which somehow found its way into my Christmas stocking. Its variety, vivid changing colours: ruby reds, greens like emerald gems, blues like the Mediterranean sea seen in Grandma Rose's encyclopedias, and ever-changing patterns fascinated me on many a rainy day.

And so our leisurely way of life wended its mostly peaceful way, until broken one day by my brother Terry letting out a loud yell when he dropped part of a paving stone on his big toe while we were out playing. The evidence of much blood and pain led me to believe it broken, but luckily, while it obviously hurt like the devil, it healed fairly quickly. As expected, he bore the name of Hopalong for a while, with a vexed expression.

Mostly unknown to us then, far worse pain was being inflicted on countless people in the summer of 1940, from London to Hull, Coventry to Birmingham and Glasgow as the Luftwaffe rained bombs and strafed large areas of the United Kingdom.

UNCLE BRYN AND GRAN JONES

IT IS EASY TO conjure up the living-room of 5 Bryn Terrace. Its cosiness and warmth - already mentioned - wing the years with ease. Seemingly always there, Gran Jones sat in a corner, a small dark figure near to the hearthside, her earphones either clamped across her head or hanging from a hook on the wall. I hear her still...

As 'e gone to The Gluepot again, Sal?

Her pale, wart-punctuated face registering disgust. She didn't hold with the "demon drink":

It's the watering 'ole of the devil 'imself, was her oft expressed view. Aunt Sal would try reassuring her that he'd only *Gone up for a quick pint now...* which, as she well knew, was stretching the truth a bit. Gran would grunt disapproval and retreat behind her earphones, thereafter humming to whatever music was playing on the radio – although she preferred singing hymns on a Sunday. The most memorable thing about Gran was her waist length grey hair, which I often watched her brushing and plaiting – pinning it into coils each side of her head. There they sat, a bit like large cow pats.

I recall, on several occasions, Uncle Bryn's return - an hour or so later - better for wear, ruddy-cheeked, his Celtic blue eyes enhanced – and an altogether agreeable expression on his face - a sort of Mona Lisa smile I was familiar with, and he'd beam at me and pat my head harder than intended...

There's a lovely gel you are! He would say, and press a sixpenny piece into my hand. I never minded when he went to The Gluepot. If Terry was around, he repeated the process, adding that he was *A lovely boyo!* Gran Jones would tut and give him a look of disdain that could freeze rain. One evening, I remember writing my name inside a new autograph book (all the rage at the time). Uncle Bryn, nicely mellowed, said *Give it by year,* and borrowing my pen, wrote:-

> *A potato is a potato*
> *A cabbage is a cabbage*
> *But a pea is a relief...*

He signed it *Uncle Bryn,* and asking me to read it out loud (which I did, blushing), laughed uproariously at his own, earthy humour. His mother said *Ach-a-fi* (Disgusting). However, apart from school friends' good wishes, a crude poem or odd remarks, I don't recall finding anyone famous to sign my autograph book, although I did, later, write to the famous skater Sonja Heini and she sent me a lovely photograph of herself in a beautiful dress, which I treasured for years.

On another, beer-fuelled, evening (Uncle Bryn was usually gently rather than roaring drunk, and I never saw him acting belligerently) he picked up the Merthyr Express, sat by the fire, and briefly scanning it as usual, guffawed and said:

*Yer, listen to this now – 'An ARP warden from Abercanaid was checkin' the 'ouses in 'is area one night, when an occupant of one 'ouse – a certain Mrs Jones (*no relative) a*ppeared in answer to 'is knock*

'I've made the front all tidy, Mr. Lewis' she said, forgettin' the bedroom light blazin' away at the back. In reply, the wag of a warden tutted, and pointin' an accusin' finger at the rear of the 'ouse, said 'You see, Mrs. Jones, 'Itler isn't particular whether 'e comes round the front or the back!'

That made even Gran Jones smile. We all giggled, thinking it a funny story.

Uncle Bryn, short in stature and with dark hair, first worked at the coal face of one of the mines, as did some of his contemporaries - although the majority were down in that dark, dangerous underworld digging coal - the thought of which always filled me with dread. Due to ill health (coal-dust induced), he then joined his only son, Will John, by working at the Horricks drinks factory for a while – the mention of which had us dreaming of Cream Soda and ice cream and Dandelion & Burdock. Then, Gran Jones did something quite unique, which caused a great stir on the mountain. She dipped into her savings and bought her son A BUS!

'A bus if you please, mun. Fancy 'er 'aving all that money!' was overheard, whispered in back yards and over fences. It wasn't every day that Mountainarian mothers bought buses for their sons. It was a single decker, colliery bus, and Uncle Bryn enjoyed driving the miners to and from the pit for a few years. Terry and I used to beg for rides on that wonderfully coal-smelly bus, for the aroma was seductive and addictive.

I dimly recall one time when Mum came to see us for a long weekend and persuaded my put-upon aunt to buy a modern cooker, as the black-leaded stove was hard work. After demurring for several hours, Aunt Sal gave in and she and Mum went to buy said cooker. Well, Gran Jones was hopping mad – thinking modern appliances unfit for her house. However the stove was installed and several neighbours came in to gaze longingly at it. Mum told me that it was the very first modern cooker in Mountain Hare, and human nature being what it is, it wasn't long before other housewives had one too.

There was another incident which soured the atmosphere for a while. Appreciating what Aunt Sal did for us children, Mum helped as much as she could when visiting. Rising earlier than usual on a Sunday morning, she took tea up to Aunt Sal and Uncle Bryn – which was a novelty then. Not wishing to leave Gran Jones out, she took her a cup too and placed it on her bedside table with *A cup of tea for you, Gran.* Oh what a kerfuffle that was to cause later! Mouth set in a grimace, she stomped downstairs and told Mum in no uncertain terms to:

Never bring me tea in bed again. Do you 'year? My 'usband would turn over in 'is grave if 'e saw me drink it.

And she promptly threw the cold tea down the sink, giving Mum a wide berth for the rest of the day. There's nowt as queer as folk. The only time that Gran Jones really invoked my sympathy and interest was when she told me the sad tale of how her younger sister died.

She washed her 'air and dried it too near to the fire and it caught alight. In a panic, she rushed out into the street. The flames were fanned by the breeze and she was burned to death, as no one was around at the time to save 'er. 'T'was God's will!

Surely, God couldn't be so uncaring, I thought. Of course, I was very young at the time. I feel quite mean portraying Gran Jones in such a bad light; I'm sure that she had some more likeable qualities. One time, she took brother Bryan – just after we arrived – onto her knee and recited the words of the following old nursery rhyme:

Miss Polly had a dolly who was sick, sick, sick
So she called for the doctor to come quick, quick, quick
The doctor came with his bag and his hat
And he knocked on the door with a rat-a-tat-tat.
He looked at the dolly and he shook his head
And he said to Miss Polly 'Put her straight to bed.'
He wrote on a paper for some pills, pills, pills
'I'll be back in the morning for my bill, bill, bill.'

I'm sure that I enjoyed it more than Bryan did! I guess some people's kindness lies a bit deeper, that's all. Guilt comes rushing to the fore when I think about one, ill-advised, assumption about a situation on my part. On the way home from school one day – aware that one of Gran's brothers who lived opposite the school had been ill – I was shocked to see that his house blinds were fully drawn. In my head, that meant only one thing: he had breathed his last, for as soon as anyone died in Wales then, blinds were immediately lowered as a sign of respect. I rushed home to tell Gran Jones the awful news.

Your brother Reece has died, Gran!

Her face grew even paler and with a *Dew dew* and a sob, she put on her coat and hat and without another word, head shaking, made her tutting way down the mountain. Gran Jones found her brother recovering, smoking his pipe, the blinds drawn against the afternoon sun. Did I get some verbal stick on her return! I was made to feel even worse in Chapel on the next Sunday when he – fit as the proverbial flea –stood before the congregation and said:

*Contrary to certain rumours about my recent demise… (*glancing at me with a twinkle in his eye) *as you can see I am still in the land of the livin'!* Everyone, except me, laughed heartily. My cheeks flamed as I slid down in the pew, mortified. I think that Gran Jones reached a far-flung year before turning up her toes. Sadly, Uncle Bryn didn't make very old bones. Doubtless, the mines, or rather the coal dust from the mines, was responsible for his premature demise, as it was for so many other unfortunate and younger souls.. I remember Uncle Bryn with affection.

TEARS FOR BRYAN

ONE MEMORABLE DAY ON our mountain, Aunt Alice – a jolly, Bisto brown-clothed, hillock of a woman, from Ebbw Vale came visiting. She was another of Mum's many cousins. It was more than a social call, although her intention was driven by a good heart. Aware that Mum was keen to return to Dagenham to play her part by doing war work and that Aunt Sal could hardly be expected to cope with three young children (in view of her badly ulcerated leg), she pleaded with Mum to let her foster our Bryan. With two little girls but no son, he seemed heaven sent with his blue eyes, rosy cheeks and dimpled limbs. And he was a well behaved little lad to boot: quite shy and quiet. That night was a restless one for Mum as she tossed and turned, torn by indecision. She was reluctant to take Bryan back with her – aware that it was dangerous in face of renewed enemy activity, and that our house in Dagenham was in a vulnerable position (too close to a railway, May & Bakers drug factories, the River Thames AND the Ford Motor company, churning out various military vehicles) and knew that he would be loved to pieces by Aunt Alice. With heavy heart - she later told me - Mum reluctantly agreed the next morning. Reassured by hugs from Aunt Sal, and well laden, we all took the bus to Ebbw Vale a day later. Another journey, another place, another adventure! Lively as monkeys, we children were in playful mood, while Mum was so quiet we were hardly aware of her presence.

Ebbw Vale, perpetually grimed by the local

coal pit as it was, helplessly showed us a grubby face. Deposits of coal were not discriminating and a constant source of aggravation to the housewives, whose washing flapped hopefully in small back yards.

Rows of similar houses, in similar streets, with unlocked doors (what was there to steal?) huddled companionably close. Despite the daily sooty threat, doorsteps vied with those on Mountain Hare. Brass steps winked in watery sunshine while cardinal red and snow white areas of stone told us there were no sluts within. With its pristine step and polished brass door knob - signature of the caring housewife - Aunt Alice's house was no exception. She, her husband Uncle Edgar, and their two daughters, Mair and Edwina took Bryan straight to their hearts. Tea, accompanied by biscuits and Welsh cakes, flowed as freely as the good will. Preliminaries over, Aunt Alice – despite Bryan's age and liveliness - hunted out a plaid, wool shawl: a rather large one...and wrapped it around herself. Taking my evidently reluctant brother on to her generous lap with a *There's a lovely little fellow. Come by year, precious,* she encompassed and nearly smothered him with the voluminous shawl. Proceeding to rock him back and forth like a babe in arms, banging him on the back with great gusto, she sang in a softly sweet, if slightly wobbly soprano voice, which had graced many a chapel meeting. Terry and I were hypnotised by her excessive chins, quivering and vibrating as she sang. We weren't a bit surprised when Bryan squirmed his way out of her embrace. It's funny the things that you remember.

Only partially aware of Mum's emotional

upheaval at leaving her 'baby' behind, we later left, full of dinner and hospitality, without a rush - or Bryan. Being so young, he looked unconcerned and was playing happily under the fond gaze of his temporary foster family. We rattled back to Merthyr in a bone-shaking bus. Pale and pensive, Mum silently brushed away a few tears. Noses pressed against the windows, we peered at brooding pyramids silhouetted against an angry sky, hardly the Golden Pyramids of Giza. Everything was ominous - black or grey. Outlines of trees loomed large and threatening. Rain spat at our noses, only to be cheated to slither down the panes. Mum's sadness was catching. Mine grew wings. Beginning to miss Bryan too, I wondered where our Dad was and hoped that he was safe and well. Mum described the above scene quite graphically for me years later, and although we visited Bryan from time to time and he came to Dagenham for a few holidays with us during the early and mid war years, she said that separating us was the biggest regret of her life at the time.

Naturally, like so many other evacuees who lived elsewhere while still young, Bryan was confused by having two 'Mums' now and then and was probably even more puzzled by being later evacuated with the school (but under my wing) to Long Eaton, Derbyshire, and then for a third, brief time, to Neath in Wales. This last period was at the rear end of the war. Mum had given birth to another son, my brother Royce Kenneth, and was taking a while to recover. With Aunt Sal too ill to take us in, a young couple with two children of their own, showed great generosity of spirit and forbearance by taking in a woman with four children: one a baby only a month old, as land mines tried flattening our house in Dagenham. They succeeded in destroying several at the end of our road, killing quite a few people, whilst our house was shaken but only a little bit stirred.

Attending school for a short time in Neath, a rumour spread that there was a German soldier's head in a helmet on a grave in a cemetery in the area. Half believing it, macabre though it was, we didn't dare go and check for ourselves…I also recall Ken's and his wife's (our hosts) little lad Gareth trying to feed my new brother uncooked cabbage, but Mum fortunately discovered his well-intentioned deed just before little Royce turned blue.

Although we couldn't appreciate it at the time, the writing was on the wall for Germany. Brother Terry and I had attended no less than six different schools before the war's end. No wonder our education was so patchy! But I am running away with my story.

MORE OF THE HAVARDS

THE FOLLOWING IS ANOTHER 'scene' from my past. That sounds a bit theatrical but I really can see it, almost like an action replay on film. There's Grandma Sal (Sarah Jane): she stands at the head of the table, her well-upholstered, short frame encased in a flower-sprigged wrap-around apron – de rigueur in many households –its capacious pockets holding secret sweets. *I've nothing for you*…a blatant lie. A smile hovers by her mouth, like a wasp near jam. Her cheeks are farmer's-wife, rosy-apple red: a clichéd grandma if ever there was one. She clutches a cob loaf to her ample bosom, buttering first and then sawing inwards with a lethal bread knife. I catch my breath, fearing she will cut into those soft mounds. She doesn't. She lifts the tangerine and pale green knitted tea-cosy from the pot, and says with a slight inclination of her grey, 'corrugated' permed head: *Tea's rose, Sam. Shift from there.* Then she turns to the rest of us, hungry and expectant. *You too*…she says. Grandad Sam (Samuel John), balancing the pendulum wall clock on his head - an ever present illusion - rises slowly from his armchair by the ever lit fire, smooths a hand over his surprisingly sleek and dark, shining, Brylcremed hair (a habit he has), and with benign expression, sits at the opposite end of the table.

Uncle Dai (the lodger-part of the furnishings) rises from his armchair too, excuses himself, and leaves the room; behind him an aroma of spent matches and Woodbine cigarette smoke, mingling with damp, earthy, fur. A succession of stray cats have forever sat on his lap, nestling in his waistcoat, curled in balls like weird, furry stomach growths.

They all eyed the senior, pale-blue budgerigar 'Bluey', chirping in the cage in the alcove with a hopeful look, but he died (smiling?) years later of old age. Uncle Dai has neatly folded *The Mirror* and left it on the arm of the chair. I catch sight of his shiny bible-black trousered bottom retreating, and am pleased that he remembered to give me a sixpence earlier…(with a pat on the head and a *Good girl!* What does he know?). He disappears from view. The sound of the lavatory chain being pulled –less than twelve feet away – in the bathroom at the end of the narrow hallway, punctuates our chatter. Grandma cups her mouth with one hand, turns to our Mum and whispers:

Eez off to meet 'er, mun…eez fancy woman!!
and nods knowingly, her grey curls bouncing.. She then adds a few tuts and her face spells disapproval.

Well, we don' know that for sure, do we Mam?

Says Mum, but Grandma has made up her mind and can see him:

Sniffin''ér Evenin' In Paris perfume… Takin' off 'er imitation leopard skin fur coat, ETCETERA!

Or so she tells Mum. Mum gently shakes her head, smiles a small smile and leaves her imagination unsullied. My ears are razor sharp. They have to be to catch anything remotely interesting – mostly said in whispers! (Also it has been suggested, as one of my ears sticks out a bit - nightly applied plasters proving useless – that I have an advantage and am nosey to boot.)

All at once, there is noisy activity in the

hallway – the sound of the key that dangles and jangles on a bit of string behind the letter-box being pulled through its mouth, and the front door opening, alerts us. *You'll be burgled one day Mam, mark my words,* from Mum; the sound of loud, male voices follow…Grandma frowns, goes to investigate. We hear *Dew, dew, it's our John! Oh, there's lovely to see you, son!* and suddenly here he is, huge in the doorway, darkly handsome in his Navy blue sailor uniform, a grin pleasing his ruddy face. His sister, my Aunt Edna says:

'*Iz bum is made for bell bottoms!* and it proves true. He is shadowed by the bashful, fair and slim figure of a man, easy on the eye, a fellow Jack Tar. (Edna is already fluttering her carefully mascaraed eyelashes, silly girl.) "Mac" is introduced all round and I can see the beads of perspiration on his forehead.

We've left the war to look after itself for a while , says Uncle John, giving us hugs and kisses. I can see that Edna longs for Mac to do likewise, but he just formally shakes hands with everyone. My pretty, sparkling-grey-eyed Mum quietly tells her sister to Leave *the poor boy alone, Ed!* But she blatantly ignores her and continues to flirt outrageously. Grandma, humming an unrecognisable song, goes to the kitchen to fetch our plated lunches, followed by our Mum, leaving Edna to have a field day. I look at Mac, bright red now. Will he explode? Grandad spots the problem.

Go and 'elp in the kitchen, Edna, he says, sternly (he is rarely stern). She flounces off, her short jitterbug pleated white skirt swaying to and fro, showing off her shapely, tea-stained legs with the pencilled line up the back to look like nylon stockings. *Don' mind 'er, son,* Grandad pats Mac's arm; tries putting our guest at ease.

My brother, Terry – pale as uncooked pastry, with a golden topping –sits in a corner, looking and feeling totally bored. So quiet… Mum always says *Eez there when e isn't and isn't when e iz!!* Brother Bryan is still in Ebbw Vale, South Wales, being fostered by rotund Aunt Alice: a kindly soul with soft milky skin. He is the 'borrowed 'son she wished for and she *Loves him to pieces!*

Our Dad is still "somewhere in France" one step ahead of the advancing German forces. (Grandad assures us that *They'll never catch' im…)* I discover Mum now and then quietly gazing into the distance, biting her lip. And so it is that eight of us squeeze around this humble table (festive in its - subtly darned on one corner - best lemon and white damask cloth) on this day –Edna still doing her darnedest to impress our uncomfortable guest.

Just as if he has suddenly remembered something important, Grandad excuses himself and goes into the kitchen – the only other room, apart from the small bathroom, on the ground floor. I think about the coal cupboard under the stairs and the noseful of bliss I will relish before I leave…Staffordshire figures of Queen Victoria and 'er Albert, backs turned slightly from each other as if they've had a row, look down on the proceedings with little interest from the tall, massive mahogany chest of drawers. The drawers contain all manner of 'treasures' which Grandma let me examine occasionally, such as boxed handkerchiefs, wrapped scarves, and purses. All were presents, put away 'for best' and never used. Many years later, forgetting that chocolates had a 'shelf life,' Grandma tucked one or two boxes into a drawer, until a special visitor called.

Fancy a chocolate, dear? she asked with an innocent smile. The visitor, a future sister-in-law, named Maureen, hastily declined when a rather large maggot – fat from gorging – emerged from a nut cluster. Gran's button box was also fascinating, with many buttons having intriguing histories. I digress...

Grandad returns, looking a bit sheepish. Plated, slightly sweaty ham salads, with minute - paper-thin - slices of strong cheddar cheese (our grandparents' weekly ration) are ceremoniously brought in, accompanied by a mixed salad, followed by a jar of salad cream, other condiments, a jar of Colman's mustard and Gran's home-pickled red cabbage, beetroot and onions the size of a giant's eyeballs. A pyramid of marged bread, table centre, looks about to topple over. We children tuck into our ham and greenery, washed down with fizzy Dandelion & Burdock pop. Terry eats with less enthusiasm than I. A fussy eater, Mum says that the way he is going: *He'll turn into a Chinaman one of these days* (referring to his temporary love of boiled rice). Gran pours out cups of dark brown, slightly stewed tea for the grown - ups. Half watching Aunt Edna coquettishly throwing loaded looks Mac's way, I too become more interested in him. His top lip is still coated with perspiration and yet the fire has died down in the grate and the window

87

is open a little...Surprisingly, he asks for more ham. *If there's any spare?* There is a subtle change of atmosphere in the room. I am intrigued. Is that a snigger I hear from Grandad's direction? And why is Uncle John covering his mouth with the back of a hand and spluttering? The rest of us are reluctantly awaiting the arrival of 'afters.' Grandma returns to the kitchen and brings in her anaemic apple pie and rock cakes (they are). Terry and I would prefer fruit and evaporated milk or jelly and custard. No such luck.

Your grandparents nearly starved to death in the Great Depression!

Mum told us this - sometimes embellished - story, several times. Thereafter, Gran's sometimes edible... offerings were tempered with caution, while her love had no boundaries. Gran and Mum rarely argued and enjoyed a warm, loving relationship, but Gran had one habit which always embarrassed our Mum. Used to drinking several cups of dark brown tea, Gran would sometimes let out a burp so loud and intrusive that it could be heard from across the road. With one hand rubbing her chest, she'd say *Ah, that's better!* However, when we took her out to tea in later years, she never let the side down. Back to tea-time, we chomp our way through Gran's culinary disasters, while Mac is still slowly eating a lettuce leaf like a bored, nervous rabbit and pushing a piece into the middle of his plate. To our surprise, Uncle John reaches across the table and spears the remaining morsel with his fork. Terry and I snigger with embarrassment and slide down in our seats, withdrawing into ourselves like tortoises, shocked at what we see. The rest of the party, except for poor Mac, of course, are laughing uproariously, for there – centre dinner plate - is a painting of a brazen buxom wench holding up her skirts revealing a full view of her well rounded bottom – like an oversized peach – with a bit of mustard on one cheek. Red-faced I say *Oh, Grandad!* While Grandma wipes tears of laughter from her eyes with a corner of her apron.

S*orry mate!* Uncle John places a consoling hand on his friend's shoulder, adding:*My Dad's got an earthy sense of humour*...Mac soon sees the funny side of the situation and joins in the laughter.

Who cares that there's a war on, eh! he says, grinning.

Before covering another part of my story, it seems only fitting to fill in more of the often bleak, hard but 'plucky' background of the Havards' former life in Dowlais, South Wales. I've mentioned elsewhere of their first, very basic, home in Pwyllywiad where Grandma looked after her three eldest children, took in sewing and saved while Grandad served abroad in the First World War. Mum said that Gran put warm bricks in their beds wrapped in a cloth to keep them warm and they often suffered chilblains from toasting their feet too close to the fire, it was so cold.

Grandad showed me a photograph of himself seated in the desert in his khaki uniform. In one corner was a lovely cameo of Grandma, and typical of him, he said:

I loved your Grandma so much and my thoughts of 'er were so vivid that an image appeared when the photo was developed!

I believed that story for many years…Renting a greengrocers/grocers shop with her savings, with Grandad demobbed, they also bought a pony and trap, Mum sometimes joining her father on his mountain jaunts to sell food to more isolated people. Fun in the summer but a nightmare once the snows came! Grandad had an impoverished sister, who had five children and no husband (presumably killed in a mine) and she roamed the same hills and mountains with a fish-filled basket on her head. Grandad said that she often led a trail of cats! Grandma gave birth to two more children, in between managing the shop, but she was a hardy soul, and Mum being the eldest, helped with the little ones. My grandparents worked like Trojans to make ends meet but The Great Depression was looming. Dowlais itself was a sad, dilapidated, neglected place. Gran recalls the then Prince of Wales visiting. T*he gay ol' bunting strung across the narrow streets couldn't disguise the grimy 'ouses and the 'ungry children,* she told me. There were many more wooden crosses in the local cemetery as cholera took hold. The Prince was, apparently, appalled at the terrible poverty he saw, and spoke passionately about what should be done to improve the inhabitants' lives. The Government, it seems, had other things on their collective mind and it was to be many years before things improved. In time, the majority of the local citizens were begging for food:

On the slate, please Sal! became an every day plea. Inevitably, with no money coming in to buy provisions, the future looked grim. Mum begged to

90

journey to London and find work to help out. Grandma was aghast:

Lundon? That wicked place. You could be murdered or worse...

Mum was only seventeen. After begging and cajoling, her parents relented and she pointed her winkle-pickers in the direction of 'The Golden City.' Before leaving, Mum borrowed a ginger fox stole and had her photograph taken as a keepsake for her parents.

SEPIA MUM – LILA HAVARD circa 1923

With crimson lips like Clara Bow
she shyly let the camera know
that she was pretty as the Spring
and womanhood was beckoning.

With dainty feet in tapered shoes
a long-dead fox her shoulders used –
to add a sense of chic, she felt –
to compliment diamante belt.

Fringed and bobbed, dark hair was styled
(she saw herself as vampish, wild...)
A momentary conclusion –
merely an illusion –
for she had not long left the child.

.

Denying her trepidation and fears, excitement

growing, Mum was met at Paddington station by her best friend Edna Price, and was in awe of several elegant ladies waiting there. *Wearing gowns and furs the like of which I'd never seen!*

Almost immediately, she found a job as Nanny to the two children: Archie and Bella of a friendly Jewish family in Whitechapel, East London. One rainy day, the children had long faces and Mum recalled reciting the following poem which her mother had taught her:

> The Camel's 'ump
> is a funny 'ol lump
> which you may well see in the zoo.
> But stranger yet
> is the one you get
> from 'avin too little to do!

It apparently had the desired effect and soon had them laughing. In time, Mum was taught how to cook Jewish dishes and also learned beading work - the parents being expert dressmakers and tailors. She and Edna went dancing in the West End of London on their days off and Mum's life was transformed.

If the streets weren't exactly paved with gold, they certainly dazzled from the jazzy lighting, she said. Living frugally, Mum soon had the ten pounds which Gran needed to add to her paltry nest egg – just enough to transport their basic furniture, personal effects and themselves to Essex and a new life. Arriving in Becontree, she and her family were given a new council house. Basic though it was, it was solidly built and she thought it

> *A little palace compared to that 'orrid 'ol place in Dowlais! An' the roof don' leak!* For a few years Gran looked on her new life as her *Halcyon days,* until her beloved daughter Mattie contracted tuberculosis – a killer then – and tragically died, aged seventeen, just after I was born. The whole family was heart-broken and Gran sat stroking Mattie's raven-black hair for hours, reluctant for her to be buried.

Meanwhile, before her sad loss, Mum had attracted the eyes of several would be suitors dancing the Charleston and the Black Bottom in The Cross Keys Public House in Dagenham. Suitor number one put a ring on Mum's finger but his love for his motorbike proved stronger, and she wasn't putting up with that! Suitor number four or five, Dad, caught her eye, as he had a way with words, was handsome and a 'mean' dresser: one of the first men to wear Plus Fours in Dagenham. Not that he wore them to dance in! The net was cast.

After their marriage, my parents bought a '*Very Mock Tudor house*' in Rush Green, Romford, from where I first saw the light of day, but proving too expensive to run (the house not me), they moved to a new house in Dagenham, conveniently placed near the railway station, the police station and several shops. Mum then became a hairdresser, passing all the exams, and cut, permed and tonged her customers' hair – bobs or waves all the rage - in the small, third bedroom of their new home.

Meanwhile, Grandad Sam had resumed his work as a bricklayer and became a rather hesitant (being a gentle soul) Air Raid Warden in the war, while Grandma 'kept house' and chickens. Grandad caught one young cousin about to pee in the chicken run and quickly warned him:

Keep your pecker in your trousers, boyo, or they'll think it's a tasty worm...

Apart from being 'light on his feet' Grandad also fancied his luck as a singer. He frequented The Dagenham Working Men's club, not only to sample the amber liquids they provided, but to dance the 'light fantastic' as Grandma called it. Not being a dancer herself, she gave his regular partners her blessing. Airing his tonsils, favourites were *Danny Boy* and *The Road to Mandalay.* It was whispered that one listener, who had downed 'one over the eight' suggested that Grandad took the latter! Despite his humble life-style and beginnings, Grandad was a dapper gentleman, a sweet-talking charmer with the ladies, and maintained - and with which I heartily agree - that:

Boot-boy or Duke's son, it's all in the upbringing!

Mum related the story of Grandma finding one of her hens choking one day:

She put the bird between her legs, cut into its throat, took out the 'gunge' and sewed it up with double cotton.

It was later pointed out, happily pecking away and lived until needed *For the pot.*

Brother Terry was born in Grandma's house and Bryan took his first breath in our home in Dagenham. Being four at the time, I vividly recall the excitement of having a new baby in the house. I was allowed to gently splash him with water as he was given his first bath by the midwife, and was all agog at the tiny, slippery, infant bawling his head off, only a little bigger, but more animated than my favourite doll.

Apart from working in Plessey's as a welder, Mum also worked in Ford's Motor works during the fraught war years. I was very proud of her. If Dad was King of straight talk, she was Queen of tact, and whilst Dad demanded and received respect, she was the placater and encourager of the two. So what that any of us got a "C" in school.

Well done, she'd say, *you'll get a B or an A next time.*

In later years, she was ace in the kitchen, preparing - on one draining board and a pull- down shelf as surfaces - cooking and clearing away like grease lightning on legs for the six of us. She was also as loyal as a lioness, always there with sticking plaster, Virol or cuddles. Dad was much harder to please. I was always a bit in awe of him, especially when young.

Dad was no brawler or lay-a-bout. As for Dad's hobbies, he had many before and after the war. The almost overpowering odour of aeroplane glue or dope alerts my nostrils even now, for Dad made many delicate model planes from bolsa wood and paper, winding the propellers and launching them in a nearby park to either joyously fly for several minutes or nose-dive as the wind or fate decided. The boys especially enjoyed that hobby. Calligraphy has been mentioned, and he was adept at drawing; neither did he miss an opportunity to air his thoughts on several topics to the local newspaper. Then there was cricket, which he played with enthusiasm before the war, and some football. I must also mention his amazing stamp collection - a joy to behold. Reading was a must, and he enjoyed river fishing. After retirement, he was Bailiff of a nearby lake, re-stocking it with fish when necessary, always accompanied by his faithful black and white dog Whisky. And he never neglected his garden. In earlier years, he and Mum hooked woolen rugs together, a popular pastime in the thirties and forties. We had several, welcome wooly 'islands' in a sea of cold linoleum. When she had more time in her more mature years, Mum wasn't far behind, winning prizes for her flower arrangements. She also made praiseworthy wedding and other 'special occasion' cakes, and catered for 21st and wedding parties - with the invaluable help of one of my sisters-in-law, Doreen - her hands rarely still. Christmas wasn't complete without Mum's petit fours and delicious chocolate truffles. If she wasn't cooking, she was sewing: lavender bags, covering coat hangers and embroidering pictures. No one can choose their parents, but my brothers and I are more than happy that we were born to them! We couldn't have wished for better role models.

(Superstitious persons might like to know that my grandparents were happily married for fifty-five years, with Grandad living to his mid-seventies and Grandma until she was nearly 90, despite living at No.13. Echoing the above, coincidentally, my own parents lived at No.13 and were also in a happy marriage for over fifty years, living into their eighties.)

Dad and Mum, 1939. Though you can't see, they had both been crying: Dad was about to go to war, to fight for freedom and democracy. He carried this photo in his breast pocket every day while he was away.

My grandparents. Grandad Charles (top left); Grandma Rose
My Grandparents. Granddad Charles (top left); Grandma Rose (top right); Grandma Sal and Granddad Sam (below)

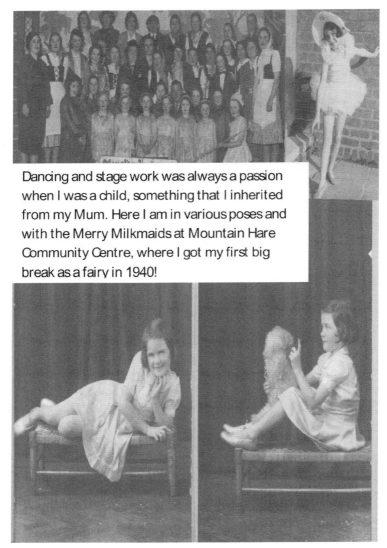

Dancing and stage work was always a passion when I was a child, something that I inherited from my Mum. Here I am in various poses and with the Merry Milkmaids at Mountain Hare Community Centre, where I got my first big break as a fairy in 1940!

Uncle Bernard photographed a
year before he went missing in
action.

Mum
Terry   Bryan   Me
1940

Auntie Sarah   My Brother
(Sal)   Royce

above: Our treasured garden,
Dagenham 1950
left: my new home, Bryn
Terrace, Mountain Hare ,
Wales, 1939

1928, before I was even a twinkle in my parents' eyes, three generations of my family gather in their 'Sunday Best'

1945: Grandma Rose holding my brother, Royce, at his christening with Mum's hands on my shoulders...

..and then just the children.
Top row:
Terry, Cousin Bernard,
Cousin John
Bottom row:
Bryan, Me holding Margaret,
Cousin Michael

My Dad's notebook, from when he was away at war. He would write almost every day in this notebook, just big enough to fit in his pocket with the photo of him and Mum. Then he would write and tell us of his exploits in France during the 'phoney war' of 1939. Here's his description of Christmas day that year.

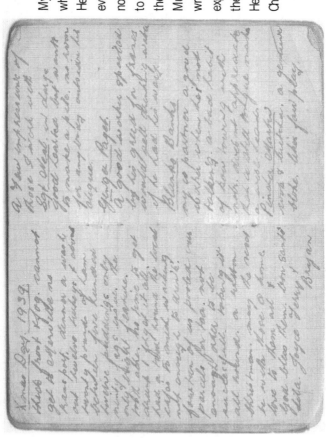

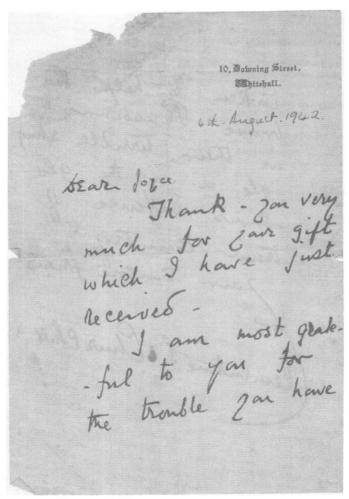

10, Downing Street,
Whitehall.

4th August. 1942.

Dear Joyce

Thank - you very
much for your gift
which I have just
received -
I am most grate-
-ful to you for
the trouble you have

My most treasured possessions are the memories I
have of my loved ones that will stay for me forever. But
this letter comes high on the list of my most valuable
physical possessions.

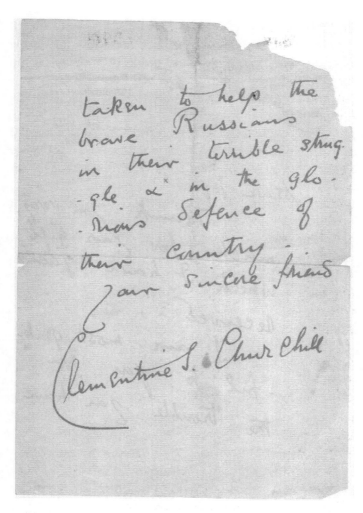

taken to help the brave Russians in their terrible struggle & in the glorious defence of their country.

Your sincere friend

Clementine S. Churchill

We had held a fundraising event for the war effort, and sent the bounty away. Days later I received this personal hand written thank you from Mrs Clementine Churchill.

DAD'S WAR

IT IS SAID THAT ignorance is bliss, and in all probability and some circumstances it is. Such was the case with us children. And so, while two of us (Bryan hadn't yet started school) were learning our three R's and enjoying our new found freedom, we knew nothing of what was happening to our Dad:

In France I expect, as Mum told us, with a sad sigh. However, despite a more peaceful existence, the ripples of war were gradually encroaching on the periphery of our lives. Trenches were still being dug; sandbags filled in Merthyr. We looked on with only a vague interest. A rallying cry went up for scrap iron. Lord Beaverbrook was appealing to the women of Britain:

Give us your aluminium. We want it and we want it now. We will turn your pots and pans into Spitfires, Hurricanes, Blenheims and Wellingtons. and Dan and Doris public willingly pulled up their garden railings and dug out their old pots and pans. The call for railings totted up an incredible 370,000 odd tons of scrap!

We were also aware of the frenetic knitting of socks, gloves, mittens and balaclavas for the troops, as well as the making and provision of sewing kits:

We can' 'ave the poor sods trousers fallin' down in the middle of battle, can we? Aunt Sal was heard to say, buttons being more widespread than zips then. Most women's hands were rarely idle for long in those days, including Mum's and Aunt Sal's. If Mum's fingers weren't rippling over the ivories in the Centre –

having learnt to play the piano by ear (an expression which always amused me) they were busy with sewing needles. And then, one wonderful day, Mum and I danced with joy as not one, but two letters winged their way from Dad in France: one for Mum and one for us children.

Mum's letter, posted ages before ours, was a mess due to censorship but she elatedly read some legible portions:

*Our troopship (*to France) *was escorted by a destroyer and the train journey in France seemed endless. We were all starving and parched.* (Dad was a committed 'teapot.') *Guess who rushed up to the engine driver for hot water when we stopped? Someone just happened ...to have a teapot and some tea with them on!*

On arrival we made short work of a chicken dinner (expensive) and some champers...but it was worth it.

And here we were imagining him up to his knees in mud and bullets, eh children?! Mum said, her eyes moist. She was so relieved to have heard from Dad, that she was happier than she had been for some time. Our letter – the very first one I received - left me feeling somehow older than I was.

November lst 1939
My Darling Kiddies

I want Joyce to be a big girl and read this letter to Terry and Bryan. First about myself. I am keeping quite well. No nasty water blisters here. Mostly the water we have is boiled, but I don't drink much water, especially when the tea's around! Tell Mummy there's no chocolate here, she would have to drink wine. I know two nice little girls about a year older than you. They say 'Merci M'suir' when I give them sweeties, and that is often. Today is Remembrance Day – everybody goes to church. It is the same as Sunday: to pray for those lost in the last war. Tell Terry and Bryan I am trying hard to arrive with Santa Claus and may it be in a big aeroplane - I'll get there more quickly.

Do the other girls like your fur coat? Try hard Joyce and be top of everything at school.

I know you can if you try. Terry's crayon drawing was fine but tell him to watch out for Bryan. I hope by now you are wearing my rosary. Try and learn all the prayers. Be good kiddies to Mummy and you be a second Mummy to Terry and Bryan and all keep well until I return. Give Mummy a big kiss for me. Bye, bye darlings for now.

Lots of kisses for Joyce, Terry and Bryan. xxxxxxx

Your loving Daddie

Misty smiles hovered. A blush stained my cheeks – for some of my rosary prayers were forgotten – chapel requirements being what they were. The fur coat referred to in Dad's letter (worn when a bridesmaid to a family friend the previous winter) was packed in mothballs and faded lavender. Even white rabbit can look showy! The wearing of it would hardly have gone down well on the mountain!! The water blisters referred to were a reference to us children having

Impetigo, an infuriating problem whereby we had spots which turned into blisters, and they itched like mad. We were made to wear cotton gloves at night to stop us from scratching. (It wasn't until I reached my teens that Dad gave me his war diaries to read, but I will splice them in here because it was the truth of what he was experiencing abroad at the time.)

September 15th
Left Debden 6 a.m. for Southampton. Sailed on s.s.Biarritz at 4.00 p.m. Seven ships in convoy. Arrived Cherbourg, France. 9 a.m. Onwards to Rueon,transport to Boos Aerodrome. First long walk later Rueon – to drome 13 klms! Earlier sampled Champagne (35 franc) pretty good.

September 27th
Left Rueon – passed through Amiens, Albert Menin Gate, Arras Passed scores of British graveyards. That made a mark...

Arrived Merville. Billeted in granary four stories high! (Lord help us in a Raid.) Fairly quiet. Regular job in galley kitchen. First issue of cigarettes.

October 11th
Day off. Lorry to Lille. Shopped. Saw 'Girl of the Golden West' (a job to understand the lingo). Swell, 5 course dinner!

13th Oct.
Wrote several letters home. Merville: nothing exciting.

Made regular visits to Rueon; also visited Pont St. Ouen where I had another good chicken meal. Visited Pont deLarghe (?) and was 'adopted' (?)by an elderly French Godmother' who very kindly subsequently sent me a few parcels, a couple arriving with the contents - jam and chocolates - smashed (deliberately?).Getting too friendly with the natives was frowned on in some quarters. They ceased thereafter.

Mum said that was all because of his blue eyes.

October 17th
Fine weather. Sir Kingsley Wood expected later. (He didn't turn up.) Wrote to Lila and the family.

October 18th
Lila's birthday. Many happy returns darling.

Dad reported finding the French women he encountered in shops and cafes more palatable than the men…and said that the (several) Belgian men he met couldn't have cared less if you were German or British!! Another entry revealed:

God, I'm bored with cookhouse food! Am hoping to partake of some French cuisine. Later ventured into a café nearby called 'Fleur de Printemps' (hoping the food was as enticing as the name). Suspicious that the meat was horse flesh, I ended up ordering eggs and chips. At least they were recognizable. A cup of steaming café au lait accompanied the meal. The more than personable waitress - a Madame Clemence Couliez - served me *and innocently (?) provided a one woman cabaret act while I ate. Seated opposite me, she chattered away like a perky bird with the gift of speech, while her mother-in-law kept an eagle eye on her back. Clemence's conversation was bubbly and decidedly different: three quarters French and a quarter English, liberally peppered with f****. She used more per minute than any Billingsgate fish porter. I explained to her that ladies shouldn't use such language and asked who her tutor had been. "F******soldiers in the first war" she said sweetly. That explained everything.* (Apparently, Dad was the very first British airman to frequent her café, and she must have found him a friendly, interesting one to boot.)

Dad continued:-

Clemence's husband, Paul, is a Captain in the French Army serving in North Africa and they have three daughters. Madame Couliez, senior, is a suspicious watchdog (needing to be with such a pretty daughter- in- law) especially with such an assorted selection of serving men around! Trying to be helpful, I pointed out that if she could provide enough eggs and chips for the British boys and a sort of French version of the hamburger for the Americans, I would drum up trade for her. Also suggesting – shrewd man, me – that she get in some American cigarettes for me to sell. (This she later did.) And so our lads got their oeufs (from her chickens) avec French fries and the Yanks their hamburgers.

And so it came to pass that in the briefest

possible time, certain edible items, more notably potatoes, winged their way from the large RAF kitchen and found themselves in Madame Couliez's more modest one. Had they been challenged, Dad and several Erks would have denied all knowledge of such a thing, for her cooking far out- classed anything the mess could dish up, he said. Thereafter, Dad made a note that:

Fleur de Printemps was soon doing a roaring trade. Clemence was sad when I eventually left (temporarily) and gave me a cigarette case in thanks and as a parting gift.

We later learned that, sadly, two of Dad's friends were killed during the time he frequented the café.

Poor old Sergeant Witty crashed his plane in a nearby wood, and my pal and card mate, Sergeant Thurgar, bought it in a dog fight over a place called Prechatel.

Apparently, Dad and his mates watched many dog fights (more especially when the action hotted up a little later on) but several were at such a high altitude, the plane's markings were indistinguishable and they didn't know whether to cheer or jeer when a plane did a nose dive. In between duties, they made the best of things and organised a football match.

At the ripe old age of forty, I made a come back! Despite thick mud, our side won 7-2!

Dad noted, adding:

The French were good sports and invited us victors to a slap up dinner with cabaret thrown in.

Dad's section were housed in a huge hangar-like building (a granary) and he and several men slept on the fourth floor on basic camp beds with straw filled paliases. (Dad said they were friendlier than horses, ha ha.) Ever alert to the possibilities of making a few extra bob, he offered to serve early morning tea, dished out from enamel buckets at two francs a mug. Not easy, for three ladders had to be climbed, but he wasn't work shy. One morning, it seems, Dad shook his mate George's leg with a *Wakey, wakey. Rise and shine...* throwing the dregs of the night before's brew out of the open window (iron barred, no glass). Refilling his mug, he left to serve the rest of the men. When he later saw George, he had a face like thunder, and was fuming mad.

Charlie! I want a word with you. You silly sod – you threw my bleedin' teeth out the window...

Dad reported stifled guffaws all around, but despite an urgent, thorough search of the rough ground outside, strewn with rusting farm implements and tractors as it was, there was no sign of poor George's choppers.

I was in the dog house for quite a while because George couldn't have a new set made straight away for obvious reasons.

Entry in November:

A trip to Lille to see how George's choppers were progressing. They weren't...He had to grimace and bear it a while longer and was not a happy man. While there, we sauntered into a bar, so typically French, I thought I was in the midst of a foreign B picture. A few men were dancing with one hand tucked

113

into their waist bands/belts, the other firmly planted on their partners buttocks...The girls sported low cleavage and side split skirts which made it very 'Slaughter on Tenth Avenue' ish. Seduced by the atmosphere, and the music, I asked a girl to dance (acting very British with hand respectfully around her waist!) But it was such a hot-house for rampaging imaginations, I kept an eye on the door for the entry of a jealous lover/husband! The air was thick and foul, reeking of cheap Algerian and French tobacco, and somehow 'expectant.' All the ingredients for an 'incident.' Unfortunately, I have nothing untoward to report in my diary!

Another entry:

Back at camp, one of my pals had a date and was trying to get out of sentry duty. '100 francs, any takers?' I suspected he was chicken anyway. The flat-roofed building was a perfect target for a Jerry bomb and was enough to put anyone off – anyone but me that is. What the hell, I thought. I said that I'd take him on. Time for regrets came later...I made a bloomer thinking that I knew all the duty officers, but a new pilot officer with one pip was standing in, straight from Cranwell Camp and itching to show off. One look at me after the order "Present Arms" and he nearly exploded. "When and where did YOU learn rifle drill?" he bellowed. I hadn't. Ordered to report for training, my sergeant said "I 'aint got the bleedin' time to train yer. Find yer own instructor and report back in a fortnight's time."Fortunately, my mate, Blanco Banks, obliged – he was an ace at drilling. Two weeks later I could drill like a veteran.

Tuesday.

Weather bad. Peaceful upstairs. We passed the time by playing a card Game called 'Slippery Sam' Hate to admit that I lost 400 francs...

Wednesday.

Received precious letters from home, plus a parcel from sister Doris; also cigarettes, Cointreau and brandy from Clemence...

OVER TO LIFE IN MERTHYR, THE SNOW AND CHRISTMAS

Accepted by the girls my age who lived nearby (the anti-tirade of words and bottle throwing incident, fortunately, well behind me), I enjoyed their friendship. Joan Davies, Joyce Rogers, Barbara and Connie in particular - plus the new discoveries I made almost daily. I was able to feed Aunt Sal's chickens until the novelty palled, build and play the House game when the weather allowed and explore further afield. With cows staring at whatever they stared at...and chewing the cud not far away, and sheep grazing in the distance, it was like being part of a rather untidy, communal farm.

I was becoming more familiar with my friendly neighbours and had an inbuilt curiosity about house interiors. A few doors down, a 'best room aspidistra' graced the front window of a house, much like Gran Jones' - between snowy lace curtains - its owner the most mature lady on Mountain Hare: Mrs –' every tooth 's got a bell' – Steadman. And next door to our house was 'The Bryn' (hill), the tiny chapel which was used as a soup kitchen in the Great Strike in the 20s. It had elderberries growing in its back yard. Further on up the hill were similar houses to ours, with dark, yawning doorways, inviting enquiring eyes, for many householders left their doors open, unless the weather soured. Parlours without passages revealed crushed-velvet covered tables and swagged mantelpieces (*There's posh!*) while other parlours showed tables covered with oilcloth - or worse - scrubbed bare. If any houses were lit from within, my nose grew longer...

Nice and handy, the 'Farmer's Arms', wetter of many a miner's whistle, or '*The Gluepot*' (*Once their be'inds sit down, they're stuck for the night, mun!*) as Gran Jones put it, was conveniently slotted in between two houses. And, at the summit of Mountain Hare – where the bus turned round – was the base of Everest or a volcano... (in truth the steep, magnetic slag tips) – the road leveled a little and a small cluster of houses to one side made up Mardy Street; a second row Mansfield Terrace.

Grey ribbons of smoke gave away the locations of other cottages, tucked away out of sight, between higher tips and hills. It all begged further exploration, especially the hills covered with pregnant, dark-juiced blackberries. I'd heard of mushrooms like saucers, but aware of poisonous ones, wouldn't dare harvest them alone. I couldn't name many of the wild flowers I came across on my travels, although was familiar with buttercups and clover, dandelions, thistles and gorse bushes. Josh Powell, teacher and weatherman, tried educating me at a later date. He pointed out ragwort, tormentil, yarrow, musk, catsear and Rosebay willowherb – although to be honest - I often got them mixed up.

Aunt Sal's only son, Will John, worked for the Horricks factory in Merthyr and fountains of Burdock & Dandelion, Cream Soda and Tizer played before us in our imaginations. I can recall him parking his lorry outside and popping in for what Uncle Bryn called: *A prostitute's breakfast.* (A cup of tea and a fag, apparently.) Naturally I hadn't a clue what a prostitute was.

With blackberrying forays in the well laden hills and the devouring of Aunt Sal's luscious apple and blackberry pies - their bitter sweet aroma inhabiting every corner of her house, a dim memory - we reluctantly faced more inclement weather. Welsh winters were not for the faint hearted, but being children, we defied what was offered and put up with chilblains and hands that hurt like hell while thawing in the heat of the school stove or at the black leaded hearthside. When the snows came, they hit hard, and I can recall with a wince the frozen uncovered flesh between skirt end and sock top! I didn't always wear trousers, more's the pity. One day we saw several men carrying sacks and twine locating some wild ponies. Had they not caught them and covered their hooves, they would have slipped and broken their legs on the ice which was fast covering the land. (With broken legs, the poor animals would have copped a bullet in their brains.) Doubtless, the clear blue skies and low temperatures encouraged cirrus clouds and skeins of gulls, or should that be geese...sometimes outnumbered by noisily cawing crows above Ffos-y-Fran (The Crow's Ridge) on the way to the Weather Station at Cwmbargoed, further up from Mountain Hare. I didn't like crows as I'd heard how they attack lambs and peck out their eyes and tongues. Horrid things. Ugh! But ice and snow were linked to thoughts of fun for us children, and when it came, we greeted it with whoops of pure joy.

At first sight of the glorious white stuff, we were like greyhounds after hares. It was a case of trap one and we were off, buttoning up coats and stuffing two digits into one digit sections of gloves on the way, our breakfasts half digested. With the grown ups warnings vaguely heeded: *Take care now*...from aunt Sal and *Watch yourselves*...from Mum, we headed for a blinding paradise. It had never snowed like this in Dagenham, surely? Fields and hedges were transformed into wintry wonderlands. Trees, benches and stiles became frosted and magical. Miss Pritchard's apple trees glinted silver in the watery sun, her terrace gleaming with diamonds. Someone found a large frying pan on the dump with a hole in its handle. We threaded it with string, and hauling it up to either frozen Longlown or Rhoslas pond, I was told to sit in it, which I obediently did and – with a fast numbing posterior - was whisked across the pond at a dizzying speed. Such fun! Our pleasure was complete when Will John helped Uncle Bryn make us a sledge and my brothers and I took turns to whiz down the steep hill with abandon. The winters of 1939, 1940 and 1941/2 were, without doubt, my most memorable ones as a child. Of course, there was a down side, in particular, visits to the loo…but it affected the grown ups more than us children. There were some treacherous blizzards which must have been a nightmare for the farmers and outdoor workers. The upper Bogey Road was sometimes impassable and the snow lay in deep drifts in many other places, making movement hazardous. Carrion crow (Welsh vultures) feasted on one or two unfortunate sheep, on one occasion, but other than the odd sparrowhawk spiralling overhead, and a few gulls riding the stormy skies, there was an absence of birds for a while. The bitter weather possibly killed several, but I hoped that those spared had gone to somewhere warmer. And who could blame them?

December.

Over in France, Dad and a pal called Danny came across a very poor French family living near their camp in extreme poverty, consisting of Mum, Dad and nine children: eight boys and one pretty little girl. The mother had been badly mutilated by the Germans in the First World War. Several of her fingers were missing and there were serious bayonet wounds in her legs. Their dilapidated cottage consisted of three rooms, Dad reported:

It was worse than a pig sty…Flea ridden and full of bed bugs, he wrote.

Continuing…

As it was nearing Christmas, we thought we'd give the poor blighters one they wouldn't forget, so I sent to England for paper chains and other decorations. Sister Doris duly obliged and we managed to – ahem - 'acquire' a tree and a tub. We then bought a small gift for each child and a bottle of perfume (appropriate to say the least) for the mother, giving a bottle of the hard stuff for the poor father to drown his sorrows. Joining in their celebrations, braving the fleas, Danny produced a bottle of rum for us . We got quite nostalgic at some point in the evening and I must have got blotto because I don't remember much until a bayonet was prodded into my chest as I was challenged returning to camp. In the morning, my first cup of tea tasted like nectar from the Gods.

Another entry near that time read:

We were sorting things out for our own Christmas 'do' when word travelled round that the King was coming to visit We were very impressed…You can imagine the buzz. He actually arrived on December 6th before arrangements were complete and was given a hand set by the Controller with which to call up the Section Leader of 87Squadron. Unfortunately, their call sign was 'Pansy' and what with the impediment in his speech, it was rather embarrassing to one and all. Lord Balfour boosted the troops' morale on New Year's day, but there was no 'bull' and everyone cheered when Jack Payne and his band arrived to entertain us. (Must mention that at an earlier date, Gracie Fields sang to us. "Sally, S a l l y") Having experienced what we Regarded as a sort of 'phoney' war, we didn't relish what was in store for us…

Back in Wales

Young enough to become overheated at the thought of what the 25th would bring, Terry, Bryan and I spent hours making colourful paper chains and putting up bells, holly and mistletoe, with the grownups assistance. When asked to: *Pop to Powell's for some sugar,* by aunt Sal, I exited at speed, for I truly delighted in entering his grocer's shop, my arrival signalled by a bell. My nose was in absolute heaven amid the mingling aromas of fruit: glace and dried, a cornucopia of biscuits displayed in tilted tins with glass tops revealing a mouth watering selection: temptresses all…Iced Gems, Garibaldi, custard creams, and chocolate fingers, to name but four favourites. Then there were jars upon jars of various sweets: lemon sherbert dabs which made you cough, strawberry cushions, and aniseed balls (which gave the impression you were suffering from mumps) et al. The piece de resistance being gold and silver embossed boxes of 'luxury' chocolates, embellished with huge scarlet ribbon bows high up on a shelf away from prying fingers. Other pleasing 'whiffs,' rising from a side of bacon and huge cheeses, made Mr.Powell's shop a proboscis paradise, and I enjoyed watching him cut the cheese with wires and pat butter with fancy wooden grooved butter pats. I stayed in his shop far too long and Aunt Sal would sometimes scold, *Dew, where've you been? Timbuktu?* Christmas puddings bubbled under their white cloth covers in the hot oven, and I loved helping Mum place tiny silver balls, miniature holly, and Santa Claus decorations on the skating rink surface of the iced cake. All home-made then. We excitedly received parcels from our kind aunts, the contents of which were secreted away until that magical morning, which didn't disappoint. The grown ups had several hours of peace for their efforts then, for we children were kept quiet playing with our gifts: cars and puzzles for the boys, a doll's cot with enviable bedding, a doll and a book for me. Mum said it would have been perfect if Dad could have been there and grew pensive, but Uncle Bryn soon had her laughing again.

Not long after the holidays, the postman was greeted with a hug when he brought Mum another letter from Dad containing a few photographs, one showing him clutching a leek, synonymous with Wales. *Trust Charlie...* she said. That put another smile on her face. Dad reported a very quiet period before the mayhem started, and was surprisingly given ten days leave in the UK in the New Year. Mum had received a telegram, on the receipt of which she paled, and said: *Oh, my God, no!* soon recovering when she read that Dad was in our house in Dagenham and bade her bring us there to have a holiday with him before he returned to France. We were all elated and bubbling over. In his diary, Dad wrote:

In my enthusiasm to be home, I could easily have swum across the channel!

Terry asked if Dad would arrive in a Spitfire on Boulton's field nearby, and we had to disappoint him. After an impatient journey, there we were, back again in flat old Dagenham, a tired but eager quartet, and there he was – our Dad – our returned 'hero,' still in his Air Force blue uniform *Looking a bit weary* Mum observed, waiting in his mother's house to greet us, grinning like the large, stuffed, glass-encased goldfish (we thought it a pike for years) on the wall beside him, albeit wearing a happier grin. We threw ourselves upon him – like a rugby scrum Mum said it was. Silk stockings were dangled in front of Mum, small Dinky toys produced for the boys and I was given a silvery metallic, wall hanging crucifix:

All bought and stuffed inside my jacket – we were supposed to travel light!

Dad said. I felt a bit guilty for, even in so short a span of time, my Catholic affiliations had been innocently tampered with. However, our parents' delight at seeing each other again eclipsed all else. We had a wizard time. Grandma Rose raided her food store cupboard and we discovered that our evacuee standing somehow raised our 'status.'

Uncles pressed more sixpenny pieces than usual into our eager hands and everyone was in party mood in spite of the war. We were likewise treated in our other grandparents' house, just over a mile away. War wasn't so bad after all! Time always passes quicker when you are having fun and so it was then. Sadly, it wasn't long before there were tearful goodbyes and we were on the move again - back to Merthyr.

As planned, Dad soon found himself once again on French territory, facing he knew not what. He soon discovered that the war was gathering pace. As he wrote:

The raids have been so bad lately, our 'Ops' room is an absolute shambles.

We have taken over a farmhouse and

smothered it with sand-bags. The bombing raids and dog fights seem to increase with the fine weather. During one such raid, a few pals and I narrowly missed death when we were machine gunned – the bullets hitting the hangar doors where we had been standing only a split second before. Our war, it seems, is getting serious. The Germans have done their best to cut up the airfield to prevent aircraft from taking off and landing, but a new idea – whereby three Browning machine guns are mounted on a tripod and lined up to fire consecutively – seems to have deterred them somewhat. Several planes were shot down and they now seem to have given up the attempt, thankfully.
Later.
Returning to camp and nearing the perimeter one night, I had another nasty experience which unnerved me as I walked back alone. Searchlights picked up a Jerry bomber and a Bofors gun was letting rip. Suddenly, a ball of fire headed towards me as a shell left the muzzle. It seemed to approach me at zero feet at about 400 miles per hour!! Needless to say I dived smartly into a ditch...The shell was later described as 'A flaming onion.' It reaffirmed my belief that life is precious. The Germans aren't the only hazard! An airman was nearly killed while on sentry duty by a car full of officers returning to camp after a binge in Lille! I was given the same dreaded watch (midnight to 2 a.m.) the next night. I heard several ominous sounds during my first lonely vigil and said a silent three cheers for the bottle of Martel brandy tucked in my pocket. I had my rifle cocked and was immensely relieved when I discovered that the cause of the

mysterious sounds was the wind whipping up the canvas covers of the aircraft's cockpits. Not all manoeuvres went according to plan! Instructed to collect my 'dirty dozen,' we reported to a copse opposite a field and spinney where some activity was suspected. The drone of aircraft could be heard way to our right. Three aircraft appeared flying low. "Cock your rifles!" commanded the Lieutenant. "B..b..but Sir..." stuttered half a dozen men. "FIRE" he ordered. They all fired in the air...My squad looked at me and I looked at the Lieutenant. In a rather superior voice, I said "I suppose you do realize that they were British Blenheims, Sir!" He turned a bright shade of pink and retired. Oh well, at least no-one was hurt and it livened things up a bit. Another café I frequent has been closed by the police:' Suzies' – Suzie, her mother and father were marched off to the local nick. They were discovered to be Belgians and suspected of espionage. During that time I came to learn the value of a 'wise tongue'...for during my visits, Suzie had asked me many questions about the planes on our drome.

As time passed, you could say that things were hotting up in France. In fact things became hectic and chaotic to put it mildly. The Controller was scrambling all available aircraft and recalling them when he realised that the plots were phoney. In the midst of all the confusion, the Orderly Officer announced:

'The Duke of Gloucester, Sir.'

The Controller replied "I don't care if it's the effing President of the United States – I'm up to my ears In this lot!" He turned to see the Duke standing *behind him. One of his most embarrassing moments, surely. The Duke didn't bat an eyelid but merely said: "Carry on, Squadron Leader, I'm sure the Orderly Officer will show me around."*

Just before things went really haywire and the German army made further advancements, Dad later told us that a couple of German parachutists dropped into their compound. He was present at the time, and as they couldn't speak a word of English and he could only remember '*Achtung*'and '*Auf wiedersehen*' he wasn't much help. However, he suddenly remembered an AC2 who could rattle off German like a native and soon found him.

Play your cards right, old son, he said ..a*nd you'll land yourself a plum job.*

The AC2 was immediately promoted to Sergeant and official interpreter, which pleased Dad – and him – no end. Another entry read:

The farmhouse became unbearably overcrowded with all personnel working in Ops transferred there. I thought it a sure target for Jerry so had a look for another hut for Banksey and me to sleep in. The one I found was designed to house forty people so there was plenty of elbow room. (George was about the only one who knew of my and Banksey's sleeping arrangements.) A few days later, Banksey and I had a ' heavy' evening in the village, drinking far too many toasts to those back home and 'ones for the road.' We toddled...back to camp and turned in. Somehow, something about the next morning wasn't quite right – it was eerily quiet. Banksey went to the *`cookhouse and found NO ONE! The guardroom was empty too.*

Our hut was missed because it was supposed to be empty! It dawned on our thick heads: the whole camp had been evacuated. George Gardner was unable to warn us as he didn't know our whereabouts. In the confusion, he must have assumed we were in the sea of blue uniforms in front or behind him. We managed to find some food and checked the farmhouse. It was a right mess – everyone had obviously left in an awful hurry...Banksey and I exchanged uneasy glances.

A late entry, which should have been made earlier, confirmed that Dad had met Clemence's husband, Paul, for the first time. They exchanged gifts – American cigarettes for Paul, red Algerian wine for Dad. He said that it tasted like he imagined red ink would. Dad was promoted to A/C 1 around about that time. When it was Dad's birthday on January 21st Clemence bought him a signet ring. It struck me that she must have been very fond of our Dad. During this period, treasured letters from home arrived and another parcel from his sister Doris.

Back to Dad and Banksey's dilemma about being stranded...they naturally grew uneasy about the advancing Germans, realising that they were in a quandary.

However Dad noted that it could have been worse because Banksey was one of the best scroungers and fiddlers in the RAF, bar none.

Resourceful was his middle name, Dad commented. With a *"Don't panic, Charlie,"* he left briefly, only to return with a fresh-water carrier!

We topped it up with petrol and oil (luckily available) put our baggage aboard and headed for Lille. Our muzzy heads were bombarded with doubts as to the whys and wherefores of the situation we found ourselves in. We arrived in Lille and had a hot meal. En route, we had passed several convoys of troops heading in the direction of Ostende, Belgium, but could only surmise as to what was actually happening. What we didn't know was that the convoy's ultimate destination was Dunkirk.

When we checked on Clemence and her family's welfare en route, we found her in a terrible state. "The Bosche are coming, the Bosche are coming," she kept repeating over and over. Doing our best to reassure her, we had tea. After calming down, she made a suggestion that really staggered me.

"Stay with me, Sharlie!" she begged, clutching my arm. "I have a sister living in the South of France" (It was the first time I had heard of her existence.) "…. We could live there together." She continued. I gently explained that, although I was fond of her, I dearly loved my wife and children back home.

After a while, she nodded with tears in her eyes and said that she understood. I was naturally flattered and moved but still taken aback. I promised to call and say goodbye if we had to move on, if there was time. And time was of the essence.

We discovered that the granary where we had stayed before was deserted and made our way to the airfield where we met George Gardner. He had several questions to ask. He also told us that the situation was getting desperate and that an evacuation would take place during the afternoon of the next day. A loft section of some stables - surprisingly clean and modern - roof intact, was to house us for the night. All British troops were to leave France as soon as possible. A few of us managed to spend the evening with Clemence at the café and she wanted to give me a radio, which I couldn't accept, so she gave us all cigarettes and a bottle of cognac each. We danced together and that was the last time I saw her. A sad ending to a brief, wonderful friendship.

The next morning, we awoke to the sound of anti-aircraft guns or bombs, or both? We weren't sure...All that wine! Ignoring hangovers and scrambling our senses, we hastily recovered as all hell let loose and I yelled an urgent "Come on" to George. We made a frantic dash from the approaching bombers which were close to the airfield, pulling on our clothes as we went. The petrol dumps all around didn't exactly boost our confidence. We headed for a field which seemed clear of danger and promised shelter by a hedge. We were joined by a couple of younger airmen with the same idea who, being faster on their feet, passed us as the action started. That ditch and hedge seemed a mile away...George was practially breathing down my neck. All at once, he pitched forward onto his face. Poor old George has bought it, I thought - he's stopped a shell splinter and looked down at him, aghast – bombers forgotten – as he slowly raised his head. I stood transfixed. Then the look on my anxious face widened and split into a rib-bursting laugh. George had put his foot into a fresh

129

cow-pat and pitched face first into another...He looked a picture - a blend of green and brown shit, from his boots to the top of his head. I staggered those last few yards and collapsed, still laughing on the ground.

"That was about as good a time as any to go – laughing!!" I said, but George was not amused. I wiped the tears from my eyes, but It wasn't tears that I wiped from George's! To our relief, the bombing stopped and there were several palls of smoke around the drome but at least least no petrol dump hits. Several Hurricanes were burning fiercely and other wrecked ones stood on their noses. Clemence's café nearby had a near miss. We managed to get back to the stables and George had to have a thorough shower and unpack his best uniform. Several of the Erks gave him a wide berth during this procedure – and not because of his status of Sergeant. A deodorized George and I collected our sandwiches and gear and were whisked away by lorry at the designated hour. Our destination was questionable. Never had we been so completely caught up in the vortex of war.

Arriving at Boulogne, we found the rest camps full. A vague "You'll have to find your own accommodation" was all the joy we got.

Bomb shelters were also choc- a- bloc, but we found a sea wall which promised at least some cover, and managed to scrounge sandbags to provide shelter and protection should we be attacked again. The dock installations and ships bobbing about in the harbour made me exceedingly uneasy but it was a case of Hobson's choice. It wasn't much fun camping in that damp, draughty spot. Pitch dark as it was later, it was eerie watching the searchlights probe the night sky, which reverberated from continual ack-ack. One of the ships received a direct hit and exploded into a hundred pieces. The whole harbour was lit up like Crystal Palace.

We crouched silent and immobile, our tense faces speaking volumes as we knew what was to follow. The next six hours were sheer pandemonium.

Hundreds of bombs were dropped and dozens of fires were ablaze. I had never before seen anything to liken it. It was an earthbound Dante's inferno.

I will never forget being part of such an horrendous night and hope never to live through such a thing again. The first respite came with the dawn.

Gradually the gunfire ceased, and with the first streaks of light, the searchlights faded away. Everything looked and was a terrible wreck in the light of day: choking smoke everywhere and only three ships intact in the harbour. George and I checked on a few young airmen. They were OK but, not surprisingly, had the jitters. We managed to forage for and find tea, and bacon sandwiches. We laced our tea with Martell's brandy and took note of each haggard face nearby. Some looked blank or uncaring, while other expressions said it all.

Amid the confusion, George sent a few Erks on a quest for information and they learned that a cross channel ship would try and get alongside one of the less damaged piers at 9.00 a.m. and pull out as soon as possible. Sure enough, they spotted a ship making its way to the pier only a few hundred yards from where we stood. As it nosed its careful way in, we saw the air cover: a flight of Hurricanes and Spitfires, and a huge cheer went up. As we made our way forward, we were staggered at the huge number of newspaper men: English, French, Dutch and Belgians, and brass hat men by the dozen. Our small band of men managed to get aboard, and at 10.a.m., breathed a sigh of relief as we took our leave of France. Luck was with us as we had air cover all the way to Dover. "Thank the Lord for the brass hats on board," I whispered to George.

We had escaped in the nick of time. The mass evacuation of Dunkirk was soon to follow.

AUNT FLORRIE

DAD HAD MANY COUSINS - several still living in the East End of London – and a colourful bunch they were too, none more so than my favoured Aunt Florrie.

Accompanied by either, Mum, Dad, Aunt Doris or Grandma Rose, each visit to her tiny house was a special event, and I visited her several times over the early years before, during and after the war. A furrier by trade, Aunt Florrie (Flo to her sisters) made fur coats and stoles for the more affluent (often "knocking a bit off" for good or favourite clients, or giving the fruits of her labour to sometimes deserving, sometimes not…relatives or needy friends). She endured the Blitz; braved several near misses, and suffered much hardship in her life. The following is a brief cameo which, hopefully, gives a glimpse of her special character.

There she sits, my Aunt Florrie – upturned lip corners sending smiles to her brown eyes (shade like wallflowers) – just like always. And just like always, bobby pins prove poor anchorage for grey wisps of hair escaping from a loose bun at the nape of her neck. Deftly sewing yet another silk lining into yet another limp, glassy-eyed silver or ginger fox stole (evoking sadness on my part) her eager, fluid chatter is punctuated by giggles and laughs. She is better than a dozen happy pills. Suddenly her face grows serious.

*An f****** doodle-bug wiped out a third of the Websters in the next road,   Charl…Direct hit. Poor buggers didn't stand a chance!*

Dad sympathises but doesn't raise an eyebrow.

Neither do I. With not a clue what her curses mean, I accept her fruity language as the norm. Not many sentences pass Aunt Florrie's lips without being embellished thus. Especially once the Blitz started and houses fell like nine pins around her, resulting in a heavy loss of life.

Rising – leaving a wake of moth-ball aroma – the perpetual tape measure (in lieu of pearls) dangling over her ample breasts, she pinches my cheek affectionately, presses money into my hand:

Fetch a kuchen ring for tea from Gradinski's there's a love, and keep the change. Treat yourself to the pictures.

Returning from my errand, I find a near Bacchanalian table (replete with offerings of the 'gold stuff' as aunt called it) groaning with ham on the bone, smoked salmon, cream cheese, bagels and more. (There is talk of a black market - whatever or wherever that is.)

The near burnt out kettle is soon back on the hob. (*Pop for you, love?*) No one leaves Aunt Florrie's tiny house thirsty, hungry or poor. Quite large, stuffed envelopes are thrust into her two "struggling" sisters' pockets occasionally, with a finger to her lips. So she has to stay up all night to make yet another musquash coat or silver fox stole for the well-heeled. And isn't that the truth.

Her sandwiched house: cluttered, warm (crackling fire always in the grate) and welcoming, sits just off the Commercial Road, in the East End of London. She has a spoiled, illegitimate son and a mysterious lodger called Albert. She continues dispensing love and favours in all guises like a super-efficient vending machine with a large heart, well into her seventies, her particular mould rare.

At the war's end, I was given the huge (to me) responsibility of taking a fair sum of money - sewed into an inner pocket of my coat - payment for a fur stole, possibly the black moleskin which Dad bought Mum as a special treat, to Aunt Florrie's house. This meant a long journey on an electric train to the East End of London and a short walk to the Commercial Road from Mile End station. It marked a positive feeling of being grown up, although I was only twelve or thirteen.

If there are such beings as angels, you can bet Aunt Florrie's making them cups of tea, and is busy sewing fur stoles to keep them warm! Special people stay with you forever.

"PENCOEDCAE" & MURDER MOST FOUL

ONCE THE NOVEL DELIGHTS linked to ice and snow palled a little: constantly numb fingers and toes were no joke – and freezing rain was a no no – we looked forward to warmer climes. Introduced to Spring and Pencoedcae (head/wood/field) quickly adopted as "our wood," where soft 'lamb's tails' from the 'pussy-willow tree' brushed my cheek and the delicate wood anemone or 'windflower' grew, we welcomed its simple delights and soon forgot the former harsh conditions.

Pencoedcae – tucked away behind Boulton's place (the slaughterhouse owner's house) - could have covered an acre or even two, but it was the content rather than the size that I recall. Virginal snowdrops grew there and bluebells the colour of the Spring sky. I heard – or registered – my first cuckoo call there and listened to the soft murmur of a tiny stream. Also a first, I gently handled pale turquoise, speckled birds' eggs before returning them to their nest, and was later disgusted to hear that some boys had stolen them!

However, gruesome stories written by The Brothers Grimm were increasingly honing my burgeoning imagination, so if dusk was approaching when I explored Pencoedcae, I'd look behind me at any slight noise that wind disturbance created, and conjure up an ancient Pict or other woad-painted warrior waiting behind a tree or bush brandishing an axe, and my friend Joan Davies would make ghoulish noises which sent my heart racing, and lead me to also wondering about the Welsh dragon.

Come on, mun – there's slow you are, she would urge me on. But when the light was bright, curiosity was uppermost and I would delight in finding all sorts of natural treasures: a soft feather or an unusual stone, or a leaf to press. Plus wild flowers to place in water-filled tin cans. In school, we were to learn of many superstitions which were handed down the generations, such as not allowing the blossom of the hawthorn tree into the house, which I thought a shame, and we skipped to:

> The oak before the ash
> And we shall have a splash
> The ash before the oak
> And we shall have a soak.
> Years later, I wrote the following poem.

PENCOEDCAE

My once favoured spot
carpeted, adorned by green,
is recognised by different clothing,
no longer fruitful, magical, serene.

Carpeted by cold, hard concrete,
bluebells no longer there reside;
pussy willow is a stranger –
pushed aside by time's strong tide.

Yet still my enchanted wood is clearly etched,
forever dear and bold;
memories of cuckoo, sparkling stream –

all I treasure, hold.

The stream whispered secrets as it passed
and Puck played on its grassy banks;
thistledown fairies lightly danced.
For childish joys I now give thanks.

As a counter balance to such innocent pleasures, the only murder we were familiar with was that caused by war, and fortunately that was an abstract concept which happened elsewhere, most of it outside the parameters of our knowing, so when we heard of a murder being committed practically in our midst, our eager ears pricked up.

We were in the living-room one day, when I heard Uncle Bryn speak of it to Aunt Sal. My face grew animated and my mouth must, surely, have opened.

*What do you think, Sal, that Charlie 'Owells –
'e don' live far from year, 'as killed 'is lodger. Bertie
Lewis, I think 'is name was. Powell the grocer tol' me.*

Dew dew! was Aunt Sal's shocked, succinct reply. And then Gran Jones became involved. Being deaf, she was always asking us to speak up. *What's goin' on Bryn?* she demanded. And so he repeated the dreadful news, forgetting that Terry and I were ear-wigging like mad. I mean, a MURDER!

Always quick to see women as '*Hussies,*' on discovering that Charlie Howells hit his lodger over the head several times with a hammer for flirting with his wife, Gran said *She probably led 'im on*...pursing her lips tightly. But Aunt Sal, who would have made a brilliant Defense Lawyer, sprang to the woman's aid, and told her not to jump to hasty conclusions. At that point in the conversation, Uncle Bryn, suddenly aware of us listening, gestured to Aunt Sal who quickly clammed up. Terry and I were left high and dry wanting to find out more about the dastardly crime, but apart from later hearing that the murderer had been imprisoned *For a very long time,* it was many decades before I read an account of it in the Merthyr Express.

That night, aware of the wavering candle and leaping shadows as I went to bed, my imagination further fanned by yet another dark or violent story from the pen of either Jacob or Wilhelm Grimm – what an appropriate surname - I had a nightmare. Aunt Sal apparently found me half out of bed, still asleep, with the sheet wrapped around my neck. It could have been the unforgettable one of two witches, tying bricks to my feet and throwing me in a water tank to drown! At least I was still in possession of my tongue, for I can recall reading another of their horrific stories which mentioned a goblin or evil imp who delighted in removing children's tongues! Sleep tight little ones...

Was that the night, I wonder, when a neighbour's shed - almost directly behind Aunt Sal's house - caught fire? The owner was a pipe smoker, and it was thought that he had accidentally set fire to it himself. As the blaze – a fierce one – started late one night, Terry and I awoke thinking that, either the war had arrived at our back door, or we were about to go to hell! It caused quite a kerfuffle, and the shed being full of books and other papers, there was little left to gawp at in the sanity of daylight! In the morning air tiny pieces of paper drifted willy nilly like little brown moths.

DANCING SCHOOL
DAY SCHOOL AND FREEDOM

ALTHOUGH IT WAS A BIT of a shock having to say au revoir to Mum, Aunt Sal was a stalwart carer and did her utmost to make Terry and me happy. She reassured us that the separation was only a temporary one, and while I think that she favoured Terry over me (he being very good and so quiet), she and I got on famously, and she found the time to take me down town to Merthyr's picture houses now and then. I can vividly recall sobbing fit to bust when actor/singer Nelson Eddie – killed in a sword fight I believe – sang down from heaven to Jeannette McDonald: *'I'll see you again...'* The film? *"Bitter Sweet."* I was so moved I thought that my heart would surely break. Tears also trickled down my cheeks during a particularly poignant scene in a film about Lord Nelson and his mistress Lady Hamilton. (It was said that Lord Nelson himself stayed at the old "Star Inn" in Merthyr.) I'm still a sucker for poignant moments in films and books.

By then, I had become used to our new school, Twynrodyn, which was an unprepossessing brick building, with a shelter in its yard where I played two balls up the wall while reciting:

"One, two, three a lara, I see Auntie Clara..." with the other children; skipped and ran. One favourite game was acting out the story of Robin Hood and I was sometimes allowed to be Maid Marion. I admit to being a bit – OK a lot – of a dreamer, and was a clod at maths and geography, while loving reading, story

141

telling, spelling and history, and especially hand-writing itself. There is just something special about the forming of words on blank sheets of paper.

One particular, painful, incident stands out whilst attending the mountain school. Brought up – until then – as a 'good Catholic,' I had a pronounced sense of right and wrong and telling the truth was important to me. Even the smallest fib would weigh heavy on my conscience. One morning during prayers *'Deliver us from temptation...'* an unfriendly wasp crawled into one ear and stung me.

*Oh, miss...*I sobbed as a blue bag was applied to the painful area.

Do you think the devil sent it?

She just laughed and assured me that he hadn't but I remembered frightening Terry by making weird shadow figures/animals on the wall in the candle-light of our bedroom...I had surely erred from *'The path'*...

I was soon taught the history of Merthyr Tydfil and found it fascinating, if tragic. Around about the 5th century, a Christian Princess named Tydfil, the daughter of a chieftain named Brychan, together with her husband and children, were murdered by maurauding Picts near where the Parish church still stands today. The shrine of St Tydfil became a place of pilgrimage, and in about 1140 someone called Iestyn ap Gwrgant established the Waun Fair and the hamlet grew to accommodate visiting merchants and pedlars selling their wares. A few Inns were erected for the purpose and the population multiplied. Sadly, because of coal mining and the discovery of rich iron ore deposits, Merthyr and the surrounding countryside, lost some of its former pastoral beauty. Geographically, Merthyr Tydfil lies at the head of the Taf Valley and shares a southerly access to the glorious Brecon Beacons National Park and its neighbour the Cynon valley.

On one memorable day, I was taken to visit the 'Jewel in Merthyr's Crown' Cyfarthfa Castle, a few miles from Mountain Hare. I can vividly recall the pungent aroma of newly mown grass under my feet and the huge, beautiful expanse of parkland and many mature trees surrounding me as I explored. I cannot drum up a vision of the castle's interior but know that, today, the ground floor houses a museum, while the rest of the impressive building serves as a Secondary school. In the past, the grand, castellated mansion overlooked the immensely successful ironworks. It was said that one face of the main clock (the one visible to the workers) remained blank in the 'old days'…

Nowadays, you can admire an extensive and fine collection of art or stroll through the galleries and be reminded of Richard Trevithick's Penydarren locomotive of 1804, the first locomotive to pull a load along rails. You can also find the first steam whistle there and the first voting ballot box. Home to William Crawshay II and family at the time, Carfarthfa Castle serves as a reminder of the Ironmaster's dominance over the town and the wealth the iron industry brought to the area.

Now allowed to venture further afield – after small sermons as to behave and watch the road - I walked down to Merthyr town, having been formally introduced to Miss Patricia Lewis by Mum before she left for Becontree to stay with Grandma, and *Do war work.* Having just turned eight, although sad, another part of me felt grown up and trustworthy. However, there was one building – a certain, forsaken house near to the old synagogue, a real wreck of a place, I was wary of. My imagination was well honed by a recent book I had read called *'The Lady in White'* (I believe there are a few books with that title?). Anyhow, I became obsessed with the thought that I'd see the pale and ghostly lady emerge from that abandoned building, which wasn't far from Miss Lewis's studio. One day, as I was passing on the other side of the road, an 'arm' of rose patterned wallpaper suddenly waved to me through a broken window and nearly frightened me to death! However, once inside Pat's studio, I felt safe, and delighted in her teaching me those first basic steps, progressing to 'soft shoe dancing,' a precursor to block toe ballet, for which I was trained later in the war in the famous Tiller Girls Dance school in the West End of London. However, with doodle-bugs and rockets still falling from the skies, Mum put a stop to lessons as it was thought too dangerous. I never did get to dance on the tops of my toes but the training was rigorous! In hindsight, it was just as well, as I didn't grow taller than five foot, two inches so would have been too much of a 'short arse' to be in one of their loftier chorus lines at The Palladium, for they taught me tap dancing as well as ballet. Meanwhile, I was as happy as a lark tap dancing and prancing around various stages in Merthyr. Pat Lewis, my teacher, was the fair-haired, pretty daughter of a local solicitor and his flamboyant, Bohemian-looking wife. Their home (double fronted if you please) further down Twynrodwyn Hill was detached and quite grand when compared to Aunt Sal's. I never met Mr. Lewis, but Mrs. Lewis was an unforgettable lady. Larger than life, in character and appearance, she stood out rather like an explanation mark in a row of commas. She wore colourful clothes with great panache, favouring rich materials like velvet and satin, mauve and purple hued, or stark black. I recall a voluminous black velvet cape and a floor length red dress, plus shoes with silver buckles. When she entered a room, she swept in like an old fashioned, fully rigged sailing ship. Apparently touched by my temporary, motherless plight, she invited me to tea now and then and we always had the fanciest cakes. One Christmas, she asked Aunt Sal if I could spend it with her family. (As I can't recall Mr Lewis being there at all, I now wonder if he was still alive then.) Mother and daughter made me feel very welcome. On Christmas eve, Pat's mother, kindness itself, insisted I had a bubble bath and she wrapped me in a huge, fluffy towel, sprinkled me with talcum and brushed my hair before tucking me into a large bed with a satin eiderdown, like a spoilt, only child.

A toy shop complete with sweets surprised me on Christmas morning. It is a warm, indelible memory. On other occasions when I visited Pat's house, it was usually for fittings for my various stage costumes – the Lewis' employed an able lady who sewed in the attic bedroom. I was in awe of the bolts of beautiful brocades, silks and satins, velvets and laces which emerged from the seamstress's talented hands as admirable outfits and quite delicious dresses, the likes of which I had only seen in films. With excellent taste and know-how, Pat staged many concerts for the troops. Several girls from our troupe, in which I was included, danced to 'Scarborough Fair;' mainly recalled because we were barefoot and wore peasant costumes. Another outstanding routine was 'Rhapsody in Blue' when half of our group wore blue and silver tutus, while the other half sported gent's tails and top hats. (I was a miniscule gent on that occasion, complete with silver cane.) Our teacher had an astute ear for classical music and was regarded as an inspired choreographer. I grew to love many of the pieces heard then. Strains of Gershwin in particular echo down the years. One of the most memorable pieces I was to dance to was the 'Can Can' – and unbelievably – sing, was 'Paris' in French no less…I wince at the memory! The outfit I wore was frothy and frivolous in black and white and remained my all-time favourite. Magical times for a child. And there was more fun to come.

WAR HOTS UP IN THE UK
AND SPORTS DAY

ONLY SNIPPETS OF WHAT was happening in Dagenham and other parts of the country in the summer of 1940 registered now and then, as familiar places were mentioned. The first high explosive bomb fell on Auriel Avenue, near our home, in the July, and a parachute mine was dropped in Western Avenue, our street. Fortunately, it is a very long road, so our house only suffered damage to the roof and back window alignment, although the mine destroyed many others and killed quite a few people. The Germans missed May and Baker's actual factories and offices, which were on the other side of the railway, still fairly close to our house, although their canteen was damaged; and the first rocket to be dropped on Dagenham landed right outside a school in the Heathway, but thankfully not one child was hurt. My ears pricked up when I heard St. Paul's Cathedral mentioned as I was taken to see it the year before the war, and had been as bemused at its enormity as 'Alice' had been by the world she found herself in.. As luck would have it, first time round, St. Paul's escaped intact, whilst many buildings and houses surrounding it were flattened or otherwise affected. It didn't fare as well on another occasion when a bomb crashed through the roof onto the altar, although it did little other damage to the building. The Luftwaffe relentlessly rained bombs on poor old London for 57 consecutive days and sometimes nights; with Bootle and Hull being the most badly affected, after London, Birmingham and

Glasgow. Coventry was also heavily targeted, but there must have been a huge sigh of relief when it was felt, by the month of May, that the threat of actual invasion by Germany had passed.

As far as we Mountainarians were concerned, there was only one, marginally serious, incident that I can recall then. It seems that a German plane dropped a bomb not far away, but it exploded harmlessly on a hill. The news spread faster than measles, and many boys and girls rushed to the spot hoping to collect some shrapnel as a souvenir. A couple of my playmates treasured scraps as if gold! A connected story I was told was of Mrs Davies - friend Joan's Mum - on hearing about the bomb falling, had misunderstood and thought we were under threat of being bombed further. She was cleaning her windows at the time, panicked, let out a loud shriek and said that she was off to get her handbag and ration book!! A wag of a passer by said,

A bit of a waste of time, Mrs Davies. If you're 'it by a bomb, you won' need your 'andbag or your ration book in 'eaven!

Uncle Bryn retold this tale which seemed to amuse everyone.

Meanwhile, Gran Jones' son John joined the Air Force and he and his sweetheart, Betty – a vivacious blonde - decided to marry before he was sent abroad. I asked to be bridesmaid, but was denied the pleasure as the ceremony was to take place in a local Registry office, and remember shedding a few tears at the injustice!

And so another summer eased its – in our case

– mostly peaceful way into autumn, with the prospect of a 'Chapel Sports Day' to be held in a place called Ponsarn, a beauty spot a few miles away, before the winter set in. Although, apart from balancing on the beams and playing rounders, I wasn't much good at any other sports, it sounded like a fun day out. We were to have a picnic – a rarity – and be transported by charabanc.

The countryside en route to Ponsarn was tinted orange, yellow, ochre and red in places and boasted the last of the abundant blackberries growing everywhere. We stopped in sight of the old viaduct and we girls – all scrubbed (except for 'S' who was as scruffy as ever) glowing and eager, tumbled out and ran into the cooler air. We danced into a sea of waving, sloping, curly green, brown edged ferns, momentarily forgetting the adders which could have been lurking there. Whooping like red Indians, the boys followed us and it got a bit hectic, until the 'two Dai's' shouted

Come on you lot! This is a sports' day not a ruddy mad 'ouse.

Sanity prevailed and we could already taste success in our spittle. There was an egg and spoon race, which left me with egg on my face! A sort of frantic 200 yard dash, when I trailed second from last, and a three-legged race when I disgraced Peter Jones, the only other evacuee living on Mountain Hare. He called me a *Daft clod!* or similar and I was a bit piqued but couldn't dispute the fact that I was too slow. Peter and I used to exchange comics but he mostly played with the boys. I was allowed a faint glimmer of pride by coming second in the sack race. One of the older lads nearly bashed his brains out by running off course and into a tree (looking to see if the girls were watching). He recovered quickly enough but had to sit in the shade for a while, under the keen eye of our aged chaperone. There were semi-finals and finals and the watery sun still shone obligingly. At the finish, we sat on the grass and ate soggy sandwiches and Welsh fruit cake, washed down by Pop. The Minister and one or two helpers called things to order and prizes were given out: books entitled "Bible Stories for the Young" and modest sums of money. As three cheers for the organisers were called for, two teenagers sloped off unnoticed into the longer ferns and were only discovered missing at the count before we boarded the charabanc for home. They were 'fished out,' dishevelled and shame faced.

Our chaperone gave the girl a look which could have soured milk on the spot (why did the girls always get 'more stick?') We drove back to Mountain Hare, hot and sticky, most full of food and pop and some full of glory. Our chaperone seated *The Brazen Hussy* in front of her hawk-like gaze and the erring lad way at the back.

With everyone seated, we started singing *"Ten Green Bottles"* and it's *"A Long Way To Tipperary."* Wherever that was. And then, quite suddenly, it was winter again.

Around about that time, nearer to us than comfortable, poor Swansea received quite a battering (the Luftwaffe being within easy flying distance of the South Wales coast, having acquired bases in Northern

France). Between June 1940 and February 1943, Swansea suffered forty-three recorded air attacks of varying intensity. Known as the 'Three Nights Blitz,' the town centre was almost totally destroyed. A total of 800 High Explosive bombs and over 30,000 Incendaries were dropped, 230 people were killed and 232 seriously injured. Cardiff also suffered heavy losses. In June and July, it was targeted and my Aunt Sal's brother 'Uncle Jim' featured in our prayers. One man, called Tim O'Brien, became known as "the hero of the docks". A burly, former rugby player, he was working on a stricken vessel, the S.S. San Fillipe and descended three times into the hold and brought up dying and injured colleagues. There were many further raids, which were a grim rehearsal for one of the heaviest onslaughts, which happened on the 2nd of January, 1941. It was a freezing cold, starry night and a full moon aided the German bombers, as was reported in the local papers at the time. The raid was vicious, concentrated and prolonged and many civilians lost their lives. As often happened, the residential areas were hit hard. Aunt Sal was heard to say that *It is too close for comfort!*

HARKING BACK AND THE MANSFIELDS

I VERY MUCH DOUBT that, what with school, play and flitting back and forth for fittings, rehearsals and concerts, I looked backwards very often. However, I now think it a good time to write more of the paternal side of my family, for they were just as important to me and were partly responsible for balancing my later perspective on life.

"*The Mansfields*" - as they were known in their community – had had, at some point in their earlier history, a different surname and it later intrigued me as to why my grandfather, Charles John Mansfield, changed it, and what it had been. (Grandma Rose had been a *Hampton* who, it was said, came from Ireland. However, I never received proof of this.) Again, despite enquiring, no-one seems to know the reason for the Mansfield surname, so it remains a mystery. As was usual then – in the early 1900s – grandfather was 'Captain of the ship,' a phrase I use deliberately, for he - a tug captain at the age of 22 - and three of his five sons, had a strong affinity to the water, more particularly the River Thames, three as Lightermen, and one as a barge builder. As far as is known, Grandad - born in London a cockney – within the sound of Bow bells, transferred to work at Dagenham Docks. He also aspired to better living conditions and cleaner air for his wife, and then, three sons. Dad recalled moving to

A modest terraced villa, one of 'The Cottages',
a small row of houses in Ripple Road, The Heathway,
Dagenham, with many of our belongings piled high
upon a cart pulled by a horse through acres of

152

pleasant countryside. A surprise after the crowded buildings of the East End of London. The pathway to our front door was made up of attractive, patterned tiles, and there was a large rhododendron bush in the small front garden.

At the time, Dad sported shoulder length golden curls and wore a sailor suit for best, as was the fashion of the time. There was an oval framed photograph of him so dressed on the wall of the upstairs landing of their home. He looked cute if a bit girly. It seemed an odd fact to me that his hair, whilst undyed, became increasingly darker as he grew older, and didn't grey until he was in his sixties.

Charles (Dad) was Grandma Rose's eldest son, and she had four further sons:

Prince – named after a tug that Grandad worked on - Harry, Basil, and the youngest Bernard. She also gave birth to two daughters, Eileen (always known as Girlie) and Doris. Being very proud of her 'brood,' Grandma would sing their praises to anyone who would listen. As her years grew, so did her praises! However, Gran was wise enough to keep a silent tongue in her head to protect her boys from the wrath of their father when the need arose, for he had a quick temper. When younger, the brothers were mostly only guilty of having the odd bout of 'fisticuffs,' or pillow fights. Dad later admitted to creating a few *feather storms* in his youth. However - as they grew older – one or two of them became more gregarious and feisty. Dad recalled a fraught occasion when one of his brothers shot another in the hand with an air rifle, but this was found to be a genuine accident, so no one got a thrashing…Even so, Grandma had to wipe several bloody noses and hide many bruises in her time as a mother.

Being staunch Catholics, St. Peter's church – an admirable building with a praiseworthy interior nearby – had to be attended regularly when the children were young or they had to face the strap! I recall Grandad being of solid build if on the short side, so attend they did. Sisters Doris and Girlie went to a Convent school and their accomplished hands were rarely still. I was saved from attending due to the war.

As I was fairly young when Grandad died – although I do remember him – he grew larger in death through stories my parents told me about him. That he was *A force to be reckoned with* was undeniable. My own recollection sees him always well dressed (more vertically than horizontally challenged), with a gold pocket watch spread across his waistcoat below a ruddy complexioned full face. His hair was sparse then and the word 'portly' easily comes to mind. Now and then, he sported a 'Your Country Needs You' moustache. He was a complex man with a surprising mix of qualities; you could say four dimentional! First a Lighterman and then a 'Captain,' he worked on barges for the firm of 'Samuel Williams' on the ever busy River Thames, which teemed with boats and ships of varying sizes. He was also one of the Founders of The Working Men's Club in Dagenham. One day, while eating a packet of crisps and swigging some lemonade after their yearly Sports' Day, I had noticed his serious portrait hanging on one of their walls.

The fact that he was a Freemason and lived an enviable life-style, indicated a healthy income.

Life within No.6 Ripple Villas attracted me no end. Oddly, at first, it had no bathroom until I was older, but there were other luxuries galore. 'Quality' was important to the Mansfields. Everything had to be *the best,* from the excellent food put upon their table - Gran's trifle laced with Cornish cream, cherries and almonds was to die for – (I used to dream about it while in church!) to the beautifully embroidered cloth upon which it sat, and the petit point footstool and firescreen (made by the girls). Also admirable, were the Royal Doulton vases and twinkling cut glass goblets in their display cabinet. Bed linen was the finest cotton or linen and the ladies of the house wore *well made* clothes, silver fox stoles and fur coats, acquired from furrier Aunt Florrie with a good discount. When I stayed over with Gran for weekends, I would spray myself with liberal squirts of Lily of the Valley, Coty perfume and Eau de Cologne and dress myself up to the nines in the many pretty hats my aunts owned (more especially Aunt Doris), some with measled veils like Vivien Leigh wore. The only down side was having to acquiesce to one of Gran's whims. *Off with your shoes and socks...*she would say, insisting on washing my already immaculate feet when I arrived, despite being groomed to the highest degree before leaving home. I didn't mind that too much, for the soap smelled delicious and the talcum was Yardleys. But when she and my aunts felt the material (for quality and finish) of any new dress I wore that Mum had bought and exchanged knowing glances, I was made to feel like *'the poor relation.'* Mum's pocket was not as deep as theirs.

VIVIEN LEIGH

First the shoes:
black shiny patent,
pointed toes,
click-click high heels,
diamante trim –
very smart.

Next the dress:
azure blue swishing silk:
waist-band folded;
below glittering, gleaming
blue sequins –
a tidal wave of Caribbean sea –
flirts with shoe edges.
Above, forlorn 36B cups...

And then, a one-eyed ginger fox
bobbing over one shoulder.
He can no longer dream of chasing chickens;
Oh, what a blank unseeing eye!
Oh, what a dear, pointed nose!
Later, he will be reverently returned to his garish,
comfy death bed,
next to the nodding poppy straw hat,
to nestle up to apple-green
and tangerine

crepe- de- chine
beach pyjamas –
which smell of Germolene.

And now the hat:
pert, early 1940's
black satin,
measled veil –
very chic!
Mottled vermillion lips break into a gap-
toothed grin
as Vivien Leigh teeters towards the mirror.

But back to Grandad himself. I would love to have interviewed him…

So what is your favourite pastime Mr Mansfield?

Well, my dear, he'd have said, stroking his chin. *Let's see…I'm partial to a spot of boxing, after a slap up meal washed down with fine wines, of course.*

His lips clamped on a Cuban cigar no doubt…

But, there again, if there was an opera on, maybe "Aida" or "Carmen" it would be a toss up. And, if a classical concert was playing at the Albert Hall, there'd be a dilemma!

Conversely, he'd drag his eldest son out of bed sometimes at an unearthly hour and take him fishing. Dad admitted he was happier dangling a rod than listening to:

Some warbling soprano!
for he also took him to the opera. Dad said that his father was a brilliant orator as he was quick witted,

with a confident knowledge of the mood, happenings, and politics of the times, added to an earthy sense of humour. Many spoke of his fluency and wit at Masonic dinners, and other functions. If Grandad had great fun when his sons took back their young ladies for tea though, it was doubtful that the feeling was reciprocated!

How about some games, girls? he'd suggest, and he'd rub his hands with glee. He adored practical jokes, as long as they weren't directed at him. A favourite was 'marrying' the usually blushing young woman to a particular son. He'd dress up appropriately as a Minister of the Church, except for wearing a hat with a brim, and cover the lass's head with a net curtain. After the 'service' he'd say:

Bless you, my child, and tip water from the brim of his hat all over her head. He thought that hugely funny, and had several more tricks up his sleeve. His moods could be mercurial but he was often capable of much kindness and charity, especially when mellowness set in after downing a few whiskies.

Despite Mum, Lila, being *A girl from the Welsh valleys and not of the Catholic faith!* (I can hear the whispers spanning many decades), Grandad took a shine to her. He liked pretty women and his son's fiancée was *A looker.* Used to a harder life than the Mansfield ladies, the females in the family tended to 'put upon her' a little but grew very fond of her as time passed as she was such an agreeable, helpful and happy soul. When first introduced into the family, Mum nervously offered to cook Grandad's lunch time bloater (to which he was partial). She, of course, cooked it with great care but nearly jumped out of her skin when he bellowed:

Lila, I can't eat this with its bleedin' eyes staring up at me. Take its head off at once!

She soon got used to his fussy ways, and everything was fine between them. The first sticking point came when Dad whisked Mum off to a Registry Office in December 1931,

To make an honest woman of her, after they had 'dallied' in Clacton-on-Sea rather too long…Dad admitted many years later that - *I couldn't resist your Mum in her tangerine and lemon beach trouser suit and straw picture hat!*

They had been courting for a few years, but The Mansfields were not happy souls at the time because they knew so many influential and 'religious' people who would tut and shake their good heads. Nevertheless, when born, in May 1932, being the first grandchild on both sides, I was:

Treated like a little princess, Mum reported. However, Dad's family insisted that I be Christened by a Canon, no less, in the Catholic church of St. Peters. (When naughty sometimes, Dad said it may have been more appropriate had I been fired from one!)

Dad's brothers were, mostly, a brio bunch. Uncle Prince was my second favourite Uncle, after Bernard, the youngest. Prince was masculine, handsome and strong and had a pronounced twinkle in his blue eyes. He also possessed a wicked sense of humour and a loud laugh, and one could say that his language became a tad 'fruitier' when the war started. He always bought me the prettiest wrapped Easter egg ever! When older, I was bemused that his very capable wife, Hilda, ruled the roost at home. I can hear her now - *Don't forget to wipe your feet, Prince!* They had one child, a son whom they called Tony (Anthony). Uncle Bernard, the baby of the brood, was a gentle giant of a man – fair as a Viking, with more delicate features. While his older brothers loved a game of cards and did a lot of back slapping and quaffing, he preferred his own company and would spend hours in his room crafting model aeroplanes and hooking wool rugs. He made a keen airman, like Dad, and had a budding romance with Biddy, the daughter of a neighbour. Uncle Harry comes under scrutiny next. He had a surprising hobby, for whilst being a strong man's man and a Lighterman; also tending chickens and an allotment (with hands like ham joints), he could create the most delicate icing designs on celebration cakes! His wife, Maud, pale-faced – a pleasant no-nonsense woman – could lay out and wash a corpse of a morning (and sometimes did), and make a scrumptious fruit cake and iced fancies of an afternoon. She made all the birthday and other celebration cakes for the family, and my own wedding cake many years later. I suspect that Uncle Harry had high blood pressure judging by the redness of his cheeks, and when he lost his temper (sometimes while playing cards), I feared he would explode. He'd smash one large fist on the table and get very excited.

One of you is cheating…! He would shout, and I suspect that one or the other of his brothers was. He and Aunt Maud also had one son, John, as fair and shy as Bernard. Son No. 5 was Basil, who was a part-time

160

teaser like his father. He used to undo the sashes of my dresses, and confuse me –

What's that outside? Is that an aeroplane or a kite? while pinching the cherries from my trifle or fruit salad when I checked. He liked to impress everyone and could be quite boastful (although his three offspring, Michael, Andrew and Susan were a very bright threesome). When all sound craft were called for before Dunkirk to bring the troops back, Uncle Basil took his tug over to help. Unfortunately, as so many other willing sailors did the same, his wasn't needed, but he dined on the story for a while. I was very fond of his wife, Edna. While straight talking she had a friendly, sweet personality, was rarely sarcastic – as the Mansfields could be at times - and was a dainty person with enviably tiny feet. Like Dad's other brothers, Basil was a likeable man. It was never boring being in their company, quite the opposite, and we children attended many a lively party in Ripple Villa. Dethroned and disgruntled, Grandma's current tabby cat (there were many, usually called Tiger) would sit on the windowsill outside like a large, furry-eared pear, watching the interesting proceedings within with reproachful eyes as we were put through our paces. There was usually a 'price' to pay.

"Jill and Jack went up the hill," or *"Sing a Song of Sixpence"*
(If Bryan's turn – recited into his jumper. If Terry's, a temporary deafness occurred or he would pretend that he wasn't there.) We were all encouraged to 'perform.' I usually obliged with a 'Dutch' dance or a 'Hornpipe,' tapped on a board kept for the purpose.

Cousin John, poor lad, was once, somehow or other, coaxed into putting on my pink ballet tutu (complete with poke bonnet) much to everyone's amazement, not least his, and proceeded to perform like an inebriated fairy.

You'll make Swan Lake yet! Uncle Basil was heard to remark. What did they promise him?!

Aunt Girlie, whose prowess with needles of one sort or another was legendary, went on to win competitions for her lovely work – one piece I can recall was a bedspread completely covered in daffodils. She met and married the wealthiest man to join the family, Uncle Len. The son of a former blacksmith, his family had contracts with Ford's Motors and they owned a garage and a haulage company. Aunt Girlie had twin girls - who sadly died - before giving birth to cousins Margaret and Bernard. I must also comment on Aunt Girlie's prowess on the piano keys, for she won her 'Cap and Gown' when only fifteen. (Grandad used to lock her in with the piano and threaten to cane her fingers if she didn't practice.) It is easy to conjure up her deft and beautiful interpretation of *"Rustle of Spring."* Gran's youngest daughter, Doris, was a first-class secretary as well as an admirable needlewoman. As mentioned, she was my Godmother and a spinster, as well as an indulgent, if bossy, aunt.

On reflection, Grandma Rose (firm but kind to her grandchildren) must have been a pretty strong person to have endured the needs of seven children, and one questionably selfish husband. Sadly, I wasn't in my paternal grandparents' joint company long enough to absorb the state of their relationship, as Grandad died from heart failure and pneumonia in his sixties. As his had health deteriorated (he had also suffered a fall on his tug, which lead to the pneumonia, just as one Christmas was due), it was decided that he was too sick to join in the celebrations planned for downstairs, so my aunts decorated his sick room with holly and mistletoe – adding a sparkling, gaily bedecked tree in one corner, replete with pink sugar mice - of which I was very fond, and winking fairy lights. His grand-children – by then around four of us – were taken in to whisper

Get well. Happy Christmas Grandad! in his ear as he lay upon plumped up, snowy pillows, and to show off our presents: a miniature piano in my case and a dog on wheels in Terry's. (He had howled for a toy elephant, which was too large and too expensive!) When brother Bryan was presented for inspection (he was a babe in arms), Grandad pronounced him: *A smasher, but three's enough, Lila!* and warned against Dad eating too many eels (an aphrodisiac) of which he was fond. Dad went on eating jellied eels and Mum was to have a third son before the war's end. The above scene is still vivid in its uniqueness. Despite Grandad surprising everyone by living beyond December, when he eventually died, his funeral was a grand affair. As befitted his standing in the community, it was attended by hundreds of people from the Dagenham Working Men's club, from his firm Samuel Williams, neighbours, friends, family and members of his Masonic Lodge. Mum said the hearse was *Like a florist's shop on wheels.* I'm sure that he

163

left a gaping hole in the family and was much missed by them and many others.

"MOTHER GOOSE"

ONE EXCITING DAY, PATRICIA Lewis, my dancing teacher, gathered her class around her, about autumn time, 1940 and announced that:

A gentleman called John Robertson has decided to put on a pantomime at the Theatre Royal in Merthyr called "Mother Goose" for Christmas and he's looking for a suitable troupe of local dancing girls.

I suspect we squealed with delight at that point! Pat continued:

It's been decided by your schools that, if you do your work in the mornings, you can have the afternoons off for rehearsing!

Well, we'd never heard the like of such a thing and were over the moon. When she asked for a show of hands for inclusion, it was unanimous. And so the testing time began. We were all auditioned for our singing ability and I was lifted up onto a grand piano to give them my rendition of *"Over the Rainbow."* The reaction could have been stunned silence or polite clapping, I honestly don't remember. But I did hear a clear: *Next girl!*

Fortunately, I didn't let myself or the class down with my dancing and was first costume fitted for a hunting scene and danced, while someone sang:

"Tantivy, tantivy, tantivy, a hunting we will go…"

In another routine, being the smallest, I had to be dragged off stage on my bottom and feared I'd pick up a few splinters in my derriere. Jack Mayer, a light

165

comedian, played the role of Mother Goose and I became quite enamoured with him/her when she waddled on stage, for the costume was so realistic as was his enactment of a goose. A man called Jack Haig played Idle Jack and he was joined by Charles Dudley and his Midget Gladiators, a super group of little acrobatic people who took me under their collective wing. There was a beautiful 'Queen of the Night' who swung on a glittering, star-spangled swing over the orchestra pit and almost into the audience, and an actor who played Mestopheles, whom I found a bit intimidating as he was so tall and evil looking, especially when made up. The devil's dressing room was below ours, and one afternoon before curtain call, we were making tea when the kettle tipped over and dripped through the floor boards onto his costume. It seems that the water soaked his tail and he was fuming. He came into our room, bellowing in such a fury, he genuinely frightened us all! That apart, it was a magical time. I never tired of exploring the contents of the large wicker baskets holding the shimmering costumes of the older players before they were placed on rails (the costumes not the players) and told myself that, one day, I would be "in show business professionally." The feeling was reinforced by the friendliness of the midgets, two of whom took it in turns to carry me to the dressing room on their shoulders after performances. At the end of the run, the midget family (as they addressed themselves) asked my mother if I could go on tour with them. I was naturally thrilled with the idea, but Mum had to turn them down because of my school work and the fact that bombs were dropping all over the country. I saw the sense of that decision after a while. We threw ourselves with enthusiasm into rehearsing until almost perfect... and I went through the whole experience as on a cloud.

When the first night arrived, we were all told to wear our best dresses to the theatre for photographs to be taken, so I wore my gold taffeta bridesmaid's dress and white rabbit fur coat and fancied my luck. However, to our disappointment, the photographer was only interested in snapping the main characters in the pantomime. It was just as well for I had two front teeth missing at the time. My happiness was completed by the knowledge that Mum would be in the audience, and although I couldn't see her from the stage because of the bright lights, I knew that she would enjoy it regardless of my performance. 'Mother Goose' was hailed a success, and while I knew that I'd never make a Shirley Temple – what the heck – I was enjoying being me! Happy times.

DREADFUL NEWS

ONE AWFUL DAY IN 1941, Mum received a telegram from Dad with terrible news which stunned everyone. Our dear uncle Bernard – the gentlest of souls – and only just 22 years old – was declared to be "*Missing in action.*" We were to later learn that the details of his disappearance were somewhat confusing. It seems that his best pal in the Air Force –also a Mansfield - had been quite suddenly hospitalised with appendicitis. Uncle Bernard volunteered to go on a recce in his place, and although the plane landed safely on that occasion, it was later lost in action. The second plane that Uncle Bernard flew in was a Blenheim 4 on escort duties and it also didn't make it back to base. Mum cried bitterly, for she had grown to love her young brother-in-law dearly. I too took the news quite badly and wept into my pillow on more than one night. Ironically, Uncle Harry received a letter from Uncle Bernard, then in Cornwall, just before he was reported missing, which said:

"*We are more than lucky, as we don't see many raids here and everything is nice and quiet.*" Continuing: "*We have been mock dive bombing and pulling up at the last moment. I often wondered how far we would go under water. We could be deep sea divers then!*"

When I eventually returned to see my Grandma Rose, she showed me the cake that Aunt Maud had made for Bernard's 22nd birthday, iced in blue and white. Gran kept that cake in a sealed tin for many years and refused to wear mourning black, firmly believing that he would return from the war. Sadly, he never did and was eventually reported as *"Missing presumed killed."* It was thought that the sea claimed both plane and crew. As an adult, I wrote the following poem in his memory:

IN A FEBRUARY SKY (1941)

Alien 'birds' gargantuan
spewed fire – sent seagulls
scattering to hover low –
chilling their white underbellies
on the grey, choppy waves.

War confuses, muddles facts…
Our young airman
tall and blonde as a Viking
breathed his last while
"On escort duties in a Blenheim 4"
which failed to return.

Left behind were
A bolsawood Spitfire
dangling from a bedroom ceiling,
a hooked rug under a bed
and a budding romance
all half finished.

"Missing" became "presumed killed."
An iced birthday cake remained uneaten,
its candles unlit.
Death's hand is decisive no matter the date.

Many pillows and eyes
drowned then.

(Sergeant Bernard Mansfield, my father's youngest brother at 22, is commemorated at the Runnymede Memorial.)

In 1944, while spending a weekend with Grandma Rose, we heard a faint noise, alien to our ears, which grew steadily into a tremendous rumbling sound that made my pulse race, as if the daddy of all thunderstorms was heading our way. We went upstairs, and opening the twin front bedroom, sash cord windows, each leant on a sill to be met with an amazing sight. As the Ripple Road, fronting Gran's house, was a major thoroughfare, it became the route for the impressive show of army trucks, tanks and other armoury snaking its camouflaged, seemingly endless way heading for France, via Tilbury Docks. It was a major part of the build up to the many battles which were to end War World 11. We watched the awesome sight, waving to some of the young men in the backs of army trucks.

Good luck, come back safe! we shouted. They waved back with enthusiasm and gave the V for victory sign. You could sense their excitement and optimism. Then Gran grew silent, her eyes moist, and although she didn't voice her thoughts, I knew what she was thinking.

A NEW WORD FOR MY VOCABULARY(NOT!)

CAUGHT UP IN THE usual routine of school and play, but with rarely two days being quite the same, life moved pleasantly on. I was often a little late for school; Terry having left my side for the company of boys his own age. I sometimes chose to dawdle en route for there were plenty of distractions: choosing to taste certain hedgerow leaves, having been told that they tasted like 'bread and cheese' (bara caws) - which they did, being one. I did a lot of 'standing and staring,' and would arrive just as the bell was rung, except when it rained or snowed.

Faces of teachers are indistinct from this distance in time, but I was always treated with patience and kindness, that I can recall. Class numbers swelled due to the influx of mainly London children, and we were encouraged to read more when there were occasional disruptions, which I welcomed! Sadly, history lessons were often interrupted for one reason or another. I recall learning a lot about the Stone Age!

Unfettered from school work, it was difficult to know what to do first. If fine, it was outside play, with sliding down the slag tips top of our favourite pastimes for a while. Armed with a sturdy piece of lino or a tin lid, skirt tucked in my knickers, I – sometimes accompanied by Terry – would whizz down the nearest tip with great glee.

We'd have repeat turns until Aunt Sal came to the front door and called out

Terry, Joyce, where are you – your dinner's rose!

and she'd scold a little and tut at our grubby hands, which we had to wash at top speed.

As mentioned, I also played at 'House', and once fashioned near the dump, it was a case of - *Do 'ave a cake with your tea, Mrs Jones!* All pretend stuff, of course. Another favourite lure was 'my wood,' Pencoedcae,' more of a small, inviting copse, that had all the ingredients of enticement further down Mountain Hare. Now encased in unlovely cement. When wet, we had plenty to amuse us indoors. Terry and I would play Ludo and Snakes and Ladders; and we had coloured paper to cut into pleasing shapes, plus felt pieces. Then there were dominoes, noughts and crosses, spelling bees, cards and 'Boxes.' Sometimes, Uncle Bryn would show us card tricks, and comics were avidly read: Old Mother Riley and Desperate Dan standing out in memory. We also traced, drew, crayoned and painted, and I loved dressing 'ShirleyTemple' in quite pretty clothes, made out of stiffened paper. I sometimes knitted doll's clothes (that no self respecting doll would have been seen dead in!) whilst my scarves were quite respectable and useful.

One Hallowee'en, Terry and I were told to *Change clothes!* an alien concept to us but apparently the norm on the mountain then. I was amazed that he agreed but we were both amused if rather wet…when we tried to grab the apples bobbing in a bowl of water with our teeth (hands behind our backs). We found it impossible! It was the one and only time I ever came across the custom. I can only recall cooking potatoes in a fire (which we ate half done) on the 'dump' the first

Guy Fawkes night. Naturally, for the rest of the war years, fires and fireworks were a no-no.

On one day in particular, having been to dancing class, enrolled to help with the 'Beginners'(the five to sevens) by Patricia to show them how to move like certain animals – elephants on that occasion I believe - I left class feeling quite useful and decided to have a drink of water at the fountain in Merthyr town park (placed there to commemorate the marriage of one of the former Princes of Wales). It was a pleasant, while cool, sunny day and I dallied a while and popped into the loo before heading back up the mountain.

Come dinner – sometimes called suppertime - I was bade to sit and eat by Aunt Sal and after finishing my meal, said quite innocently, *Aunt Sal, what does fuck mean?*

Well, if I had thrown a hand grenade onto the table with the pin pulled, it couldn't have had a more devastating effect! I thought Gran Jones was either going to have a fit on the spot or swallow her false teeth. She literally screamed at me –

You wicked, wicked gel. Go wash your mouth out, now!

I was completely at a loss to understand what the fuss was about. Surely such a small word couldn't be that bad, could it? Aunt Sal, blessed with lots of common sense and understanding, calmed her mother-in-law down and explained to me that it wasn't a nice word and that it would be best if I didn't say it again. After such a reception, I didn't intend to! Gran Jones treated me like a leper for days. Having discovered the heinous word written on a toilet door in the park, I was still curious as to its meaning but didn't dare pursue it. Many years passed before I found out!

TRUTH, DARE AND PROMISE

HAD MY GOD MOTHER Aunt Doris, seen some of my escapades in or near Mountain Hare in 1939 and the early 40s, she would have had fifty fits. At times I was quite a tom-boy, despite being very feminine at others! When we children took it into our heads to 'go exploring,' and get a bit scruffy in the process, that is exactly what we did. Apart from the occasional unladylike habit of whizzing down the slag heaps on a piece of lino, and squeezing under the odd, dank bridge just for the devil of it (listening for the scampering of rats), I played in the street with my mountain friends, male and female.

Unheard of at home! I can also remember one daring occasion when I hung onto the back of the stinking cattle truck like the boys. It housed several wild-eyed animals – cows I presumed - destination the slaughterhouse, just beyond 'Boulton's House' a few fields away. When the wind was in the wrong direction, it blew a horrible, sickly smell up our nostrils, which made us wince. We just accepted its presence, although surely, we couldn't have approved? It's strange how the connection between the meat on our plates and the cattle in the fields didn't register in our brains then in quite the same way as it does today! (When older, I was a vegetarian for about four and a half years until ill health bade me eat chicken and fish.) But back to playtime. It also consisted of hopscotch, racing, skipping, and 'chase me.' Not 'kiss chase' though – that was to come much later. Gone were the days of sitting (*Knees together please!)*

learning to embroider under my aunt's eagle gaze, or sitting in St Peter's beautiful church - decorated in blue and gold - my ensemble complete with immaculate white shoes and lace gloves, under her equally keen eye, learning my rosary prayers, and grimacing as the incense swung over my head. She was determined to make, *A little lady out of you!* My nails were inspected regularly – half moons encouraged. If she could see them then. Oh dear!

One Saturday, a couple of the girls and I ventured even further afield and nearly stumbled over a pile of bricks, lying higgledy, piggledy on a grassy hillock. Holding back, having seen a gaping hole indicative of a disused mine shaft, we knelt down in the grass – our mouths open, our hearts pounding fit to burst at the thought of falling into that dark, deep place. Edging forward with much care, we each dropped stones over the lip. At this distance in time, it is difficult to know how many numbers we marked: ….*seven, eight, nine, ten*...? We didn't hang around there once they 'plopped' in the water below. I didn't tell anyone *exactly* what happened, but one of the girls did and I heard that the shaft was bricked in soon afterwards. Aunt Sal and Mum remained ignorant of my involvement, as they frowned at my exploring too far afield!

As dusk was gathering one early evening, we decided to play 'Truth, Dare and Promise.' It could be quite an inane game sometimes, at others it flew too close to the wind. Several of us chose Dare rather than Truth or Promise, which is interesting on scrutiny! Perhaps timid souls (I was very passive) suddenly felt daring when challenged by teenagers to do something they normally would shy away from. Or maybe they just didn't want to look cowardly ninnies. Choosing Truth usually meant telling someone they had Mickey Mouse ears or a large nose (in fits of giggles, of course). When it came to Dare, it could have been as innocuous as pretending to be certain animals, thereby making asses of ourselves. It was also thought hilarious to rap on a particular house's door-knocker and hide, or thread string through a few knockers and pull hard thereby annoying more people at the same time! How often, over the years, was that trick played by children everywhere! On the occasion I'm writing about, it got sillier than usual and even more daring....There were a couple of teenagers who disappeared, after whispers and guffaws (what was that all about?) and a few others who suggested we say things to adults that we younger ones wouldn't dare. When it came to my turn, I chose a dare. One of the older girls said *You've got to show him your thingy...* and turning to a young lad, whose name I fortunately don't recall, said *And you've got to show her yours!* Well, I was mortified. I wasn't going to reveal my private part to that grinning mob. And neither was the lad with the beetroot face, which matched mine. So, after being called *Cowardly custards* or similar, we both said we would, if we could do it in private. Thereafter, we retreated behind a clump of bushes, and I quickly lifted up my skirt, whipped down my navy knickers to my knees and said something like *See!* In his turn, having averted his eyes (bless him) he unbuttoned his school greys, and pulled down his pants

(I did peep) to reveal a dangling, thin, pale worm, not unlike my brothers' 'appendages', which I had often seen at bath-time and which didn't bother me at all. Big deal! We quickly adjusted our clothing and joined the gang to loud splutterings all round, which (still a bit pink-cheeked) we ignored. The matter was never spoken of thereafter in my hearing, and despite what you may think, I was quite, quite grown up before I dropped my knickers again!

Had I remained a 'good Catholic girl' and confessed the above, just imagine how many Hail Mary's I would had to have said!

A TRAGEDY BEFORE CHRISTMAS

WAS IT THE NOVEMBER or December of 1941? Whatever the month, the yuletide excitement was building up to fever pitch as per usual. Happier than ever because Mum had joined us for a short holiday, Terry and I accompanied her down town to Merthyr to visit the desirable Theopholus's store, crammed with covetable toys of all shapes and sizes. We were told that Santa Claus had just arrived by train (?)

What had happened to his reindeers, I wondered? We put in our Christmas present orders and probably got what we wished for, if they were modest enough. Dolls and books were my favourite choices, and I believe Terry had a thing about aeroplanes – Dad being in the Air Force – and Dinky cars. Mum later remarked that Santa Claus was:

The scruffiest Father Christmas that I have ever seen. What a dirty beard!

All we had to do thereafter was wait, impatiently, to see whether Santa would fulfill his promise.

We were snug in the living room: Mum, Aunt Sal, Gran Jones, Terry and I, on a bitter winter's day, sitting besides a roaring fire. Terry and I could have been reading our comics, or doing a dozen other things, although I have a hazy memory of making Christmas decorations – maybe another festive season – when Uncle Bryn arrived home from work. He usually greeted us when he arrived, but was ominously silent and his face looked pinched and solemn. Aunt Sal was the first to notice.

179

What's wrong, Bryn? Are you all right?
No, Sal. It's Islwyn... 'Eez been killed in a coal
fall.

Aunt Sal almost fell into a chair from the shock.

Oh, dew dew. Poor Islwyn. She wept bitter tears.

It was later confirmed that a ton of coal had collapsed in the mine, instantly crushing her nephew, Islwyn. Mum and Gran Jones, equally shocked by the tragic news, also cried at his loss. Although I'm sure that my cheeks must have been wet too, I don't think that I could really take it in at first. I had only experienced Grandad Mansfield's demise and he had seemed quite old to me then (in his sixties) and poor Uncle Bernard's. But Islwyn was even younger!

*So full of life, always singing and dancing, and only seventeen, wedi marw!***

** (Dead) Aunt Sal added. It just couldn't be true! Once the first reactions had calmed a little – and it must have taken a long time, for even from this great distance, I can almost relive the fraught atmosphere - Mum and Aunt Sal hurried to his cottage to comfort Islwyn's parents. Islwyn had been their only child. We children stayed with Gran Jones, who kept shaking her head and muttering. Before the funeral, as was the custom then, Mum went to see the poor lad's body, dressed in powder blue in a powder blue lined coffin. There was a great sense of loss, not only in Islwyn's house and ours. It seemed to hover like a grey curtain over the whole mountain. Thereafter, Mum would often say:

People just don't appreciate that coal costs much more than you pay the coalman at the door! (Coal was delivered in a horse-drawn cart then.)

Come the 25th December, happy in our personal bubbles, pulling crackers and arguing over the chicken's wishbone, busy with our gifts, Terry and I didn't notice the subdued household around us, but Mum – at another date – told us that, what with Dad away in the Forces, being at war, and Uncle Bernard and Islwyn dying, it was the saddest Christmas she could ever remember.

Note. Information and corroboration of the death of five miners or under was scanty, especially in the first part of the 1900s. However, a coal fall was recorded in the Nant-Y-Ffin mine and Islwyn's death was mentioned by The Merthyr Expresss newspaper. Tragically, pit accidents were common then and over 6,000 mine deaths are listed in Wales, although it is said that the figure is a conservative one. Sadly, over the years, hundreds more men and boys perished from silicosis and other lung diseases. It is a sobering fact knowing that children as young as seven and eight worked down the pits alongside their relatives in the first part of the 1800s before an act was passed in 1842, although children as young as ten still continued to do so for far too long after that date.

THE YEARS 1941/2/3

WELL INTO ITS EVIL STRIDE by 1943, the war, in all its guises, seemed to be a way of life. From an adult perspective, how quickly people seemed to accept the way that things changed. They hardly had a choice in a state of war, of course, but – looking back – it amazes me now to reflect on how human beings, apart from the main forces, from air-raid wardens and land army girls, to munition workers, teachers, ambulance drivers and housewives (suddenly coping alone) dug down into their deepest recesses and found strengths that must have surprised even them, including my own mother.

Even more stretched at times, were the doctors and nurses. However, there was a huge feeling of camaraderie and humour which seeped into my childhood and surely helped the whole process of separation and occasional grieving. Sanity saver that it was, humour carried people forward. There was plenty around, both light-hearted and black: cement for the bricks of survival.

Even when quite young, I read snippets from the newspaper and digested bits and pieces from the radio occasionally. Naturally, much information went through me like a colander – as I was selfishly caught up in the business of being young – but I had heard of Churchill's wife, Clementine Churchill, making a desperate plea:

"To help the poor, starving, people in Russia,"

The thought of food, especially of not having any, always resonated with me. It also reached my disbelieving ears that - *The Russians are eating cats and dogs. Anything with four legs, and   sometimes two!*

I, surely, must have looked at Aunt Sal's dog, Marina, with different eyes. Ugh, fancy eating her! As for cannibalism, that fortunately didn't register at all. I digested (bad choice of word) that fact many years later. Gut wrenching hunger was as foreign to me as Russia itself. I was to read of and learn the full, horrible truth of the Siege of Leningrad when much older. **

Meanwhile, knowing that I was about to have yet another holiday in Essex with my brothers (if the war allowed it) and boosted by Aunt Sal telling me that *Ginger Rogers will 'ave to look out!* Ha ha... I nursed a modest idea in my head which grew day by day into something quite big and exciting. As planned, Mum collected us for our holiday, and by the time we reached our house in Dagenham, my acorn was unmanageable. However, it was madness to think that I could arrange a concert at my tender age, and I'm quite sure that Mum was pulling the strings. As luck would have it, Mrs Ogden – who lived in the house opposite ours - ran a small Dancing School. In awe of her as I was – she was a large, practical woman - Mum came to my aid and we arranged a concert with her assistance. She kindly agreed and offered the services of her two daughters and some of her pupils - greatly depleted because of evacuation. We held enthusiastic rehearsals in her garden shed. Sadly, some of the 'hoofers' were not the graceful dancers Mum and I envisaged! But we pressed on, increasingly worried about the state and safety of the said garden shed. The frail wooden floor rose and fell alarmingly as the tap dancers 'tapped' frenetically. A calamity was somehow avoided and THE BIG NIGHT arrived.

The concert was held in The People's Hall next to the local church near to where we lived. Dressed up to the nines, we dancers were keen, while nervous. I was encouraged by Mum to dance "The Sailor's Hornpipe," as well as perform a Butterfly dance in my pink tutu. I flitted hither and thither. Pavlova could rest easy. The rest of the troupe did their best and at least no-one threw tomatoes (as they did in the East End of London in some theatres if they didn't like the stage act!) Many years before, a distant male relative fancied his luck as a singer. He entered a talent competition and sang "The Girl in the Alice Blue Gown"- badly. As the theatre was near to The Mile End Waste (an outdoor market area) in the East End of London, the audience was well armed with suitable 'ammunition' (tomatoes, soft fruits and cabbage leaves). It was said that 'Uncle Maurice' was a sight to behold when he reached home! But I digress...Back to our concert. Everyone clapped dutifully, mostly mums and neighbours, and we collected the princely sum of FIVE SHILLINGS. What was the entrance fee I now ask myself?! I proudly sent the modest amount to Mrs Churchill and really hoped that at least a couple of children could be plucked from the brink of starvation. I still have her letter of thanks. (see page 98)

184

** Tragically, as history has shown, "The Siege of Leningrad" was devastating for the Russian people as the Germans showed them no mercy. One million people died of starvation or hypothermia, or a combination of both. The weather was so severe, it was said that the land was peppered with frozen human mounds. They could not be buried until a partial thaw occurred. At one stage, a cemetery had to be dynamited to bury the huge build up of corpses. This hell on earth situation was brought about by a Directive from the 'Glorious Fuehrer' himself. The Directive was sent to the German Naval staff, marked 'Top Secret' to the effect that "The Feuhrer has decided to have Leningrad wiped from the face of the earth. The further existence of this large town is of no interest once Soviet Russia is overthrown." I can recommend Helen Dunmore's "The Siege" – a vivid portrayal of life in Leningrad - during that terrible time in history.

After Boulogne, Dad was posted quite near to home, to a place called Debden in Essex, so when on holiday, we naturally saw more of him when he was given leave passes. They were only brief reunions, but appreciated by us all. On one of these breaks, Grandma Rose gathered us all in her modest villa, and mysteriously, given rationing, fed us royally. It was then that Dad made a great show of taking out his cigarette case, revealing a large dent in one corner. Seeing that Terry's interest was stoked, he said: *Saved my life, that did!* Naturally, Terry was all agog and asked him what he meant. Dad was only too happy to oblige.

When I was in Boulogne, bullets were flying all over the place, and I would have been a goner but for that cigarette case. It deflected a bullet and saved my life.

I can imagine Terry now with his mouth wide open. Of course, it was all Walter Mitty stuff. Although way out of character for Dad – he was normally a no-nonsense, truthful man - he'd obviously got caught up with the temporary madness of war. He admitted to the rather large fib at a later date. I wonder how many other dented cigarette cases came into play then!

All too soon, Dad was transferred to North Coates in Lincolnhire, where he spent seven months attached to Coastal Command, working in the plane movement "Operations Room." Our holiday had previously been extended but it was decided that, as the Germans were only on the other side of the Channel and Mum was still doing war work, we would be safer back in Wales.

Before returning to talk of our safe idyll, I must comment on Mum's hectic life style. With Dad away again, she stayed with her parents in Becontree and worked for a firm called Plessey's, in Ilford, as a *welder!* My Mum, just over five feet two inches tall a welder! When she explained what was involved, I couldn't believe it. Again, the camaradarie and humour which existed between herself and her work mates helped them tackle whatever task they were given. She became quite strong and boasted muscles where there had been none!

Terry and I were taken back to live with Aunt Sal again, and - in Bryan's case - with Aunt Alice, and it was only when I was older, that Mum told me of some of the harrowing times that she lived through. Although against the rules, sometimes the women worked through air raids (and anyway the shelters didn't always ensure the safety of their occupants as they were soon to discover). One young woman Mum had befriended was engaged to be married, and her fiancé was given leave for the forthcoming marriage. The weekend before the nuptials were due to take place, there was a particularly heavy raid in Ilford, so her friend and family took refuge in the outdoor shelter. It received a direct hit and they were all killed. The bride to be was buried in her wedding dress. As can be imagined, Mum and her work-mates were devastated. Sadly the tale was not an isolated one, and Mum spoke of her relief that we were then safely in Wales.

After readjusting to our Welsh lifestyle again for a while, there was another lull in bombing in our part of Essex, so it was decided that the three of us would return and attend school there for a period of time which was open ended. And so it was that I enrolled at Hunters Hall Road school and given to the care of a Miss Dankworth. She was, to me then, an elderly lady - very spinsterish – who arranged her hair in a bun and always wore a velvet choker ribbon with a cameo around her neck. She was firm but kind, an ideal combination for a teacher. She encouraged my short stories and I wrote a very basic play about a Prince and Princess which was acted upon the school stage. At playtime, I showed a few novices several tap steps in the shelter for half of their apple, chocolate bar or a halfpenny piece. Being something of a butterfly brain, it is no surprise that I didn't progress to become either a dance teacher or an entrepreneur!

It was during this period that I unwittingly drew the attention of a red-haired boy about my age, if a little older. He followed me to school each morning, always walking a few paces behind me. Soon, he was passing me badly written notes, saying:

"I lik you…" and *"Wood you lik me to wark home with you?"*

I scorned his notes, especially as he couldn't spell, and continued to ignore him. This made him all the keener and he continued following me, making 'sheep's eyes' whenever he could catch my attention. He was over-weight – his school greys just about able to contain his 'bits and pieces'- and he puffed and blowed rather a lot, so I certainly didn't find him at all appealing. Fed up with him always there, like a loyal obese spaniel, I started giving him dirty looks, and then one day, fed up with my disdain, he pushed me in a privet hedge, with a - *Take that, Joyce Mansfield!* At least he stopped following me! It was around then that I realised some boys looked at girls in a different way. All part of the 'growing up' process I was to learn.

During this period, Jerry again decided to play war games and Mum was increasingly worried for our safety. There was one particular incident which started an eye blinking problem. (I don't recall it but Mum assured me that it was noticeable at the time.) One night, I thought the flames from several incendiary bombs were crossing the railway lines and field behind our house ready to engulf us. From the direction of May & Baker's drugs factory, they leapt high in the air so my imagination soon took over! I apparently became alarmed but cannot recall the fear. In the light of day, little damage seemed to have been caused to the perimeter of the factory, but orange flames roaring into an inky black sky suggested a different ending!

Ironically, it was my turn to reassure Mum on one or two other occasions as she had an aversion to mice and snakes. I thought mice rather cute but hadn't come across any snakes in my travels. One night - eschewing the outdoor shelter which was not water-proof and therefore unusable - Mum, Terry, Bryan and I said our 'goodnights' and settled down to sleep in our sturdy indoor shelter. The air raid siren was wailing from the police station a hundred yards away, when we heard a scampering sound beneath us (the base was raised from the floor). Mum shrieked and shouted *Mice!* certain that one tiny rodent was an infestation.

It'll only be a field mouse, Mum, it won't hurt you! I said.

Deaf to my entreaty, she took a blanket and a pillow and slept on a nearby settee.

I'd rather brave the bombs, she said.

On 'The Night of the Snake,' a rainswept evening – needing coal for the stove fire – Mum, umbrella in one hand and shovel in the other, let out a piercing scream as she lifted the flap door to the 'coal-hole' outside and stepped onto something unexpected and slippery....a SNAKE of all things. It was also averse to the rain it seems and was sheltering in said coal-hole. Our next door neighbour, Mr Jinks (and probably the inhabitants of the next street), were alerted and her saviour rushed into our garden – appropriately still wearing his butcher's apron – red-faced and highly excited, brandishing a chopper, shouting,

It's all right, Lila, I'll kill it for you. Don't worry! Adding

It could be a viper...(A viper in Dagenham?) and he proceeded to chop the unfortunate snake into a dozen pieces. The next day, the story went round that Mr Jinks had saved Mum from the venomous and crushing coils of *Possibly a small python!*

He wasn't going to tell anyone that it was, in fact, a rather small, harmless grass snake, merely anxious to escape from the rain, was he! Still, it made a change from talk of bombs.

One weekend soon afterwards, invited to visit Mum's sister, Peggy, who lived in The Heathway (close to Dagenham), we were having tea, when that ominous droning sound reached our ears. (Luckily, her outdoor shelter was situated directly outside her back door and was furnished with a large mattress.) While aware of it's evil intent, we found the doodle-bug strangely fascinating - the engine of the one overhead suddenly cut out as we all watched with baited breath. We wondered in which direction it would fall, as it started to descend, fortunately just away from our aunt's house. In a trice, Mum, my aunt, brothers and I all threw ourselves into the safety of the shelter just as the doodle-bug hit open ground in the park, less than half a mile away. The huge explosion rocked our hiding place with a frightening, rattling noise.

Not long after that incident, I left Hunters Hall Road school to attend Eastbrook Senior School, but was only there for a short time before it was thought prudent to evacuate the lot of us to Long Eaton in Derbyshire as, once again, there was continuous, heavy enemy activity in our area. By then, I was beginning to feel like a shuttlecock!

And so, accompanied by Bryan this time - Terry stubbornly refusing to leave (one of his most enduring traits) - we were tagged, bused and finally transported by train to Derbyshire. By the end of the long journey, I had more than a blue ribbon amongst my dark curls!

LONG EATON AND NEATH, WALES

PACKED CHEEK BY JOWL with a dozen other children - not all neatly groomed and scrubbed - in a small train compartment, was a recipe for 'flea playtime.' However, not having been host to the horrid things before, I just scratched and wondered. Until I reached my destination that is. Mum, having been a hairdresser and proud of the state of our hair – always shampooing, crimping and rag curling (well mine anyway) - was told in a curt letter that *Your daughter has an infestation of nits!* It was worse than an insult.

She was mortified. In truth, it was nothing terrible and quite common at the time, but not for US, or rather ME!

However, before the letter winged its informative way, we - Bryan and I - found ourselves disgorged in the courtyard of either an hotel or a public building, waiting to be chosen. This was a rather humiliating process, repeated all over the county, whereby the prettiest, cutest, or strongest children were picked first. Woe betide the cross-eyed, skinny kids with runny noses! Luckily, we fell in neither category so, whilst not exactly snapped up, we were in the middle of the 'choosing' order. There was, at first, some indecision, as many people only wanted one child but I wouldn't be split up from my younger brother. I'd promised Mum, and I wanted to keep an eye on him anyway. It appealed to my older sister standing, and I loved him to boot.

A lady (Mrs Hawkins) took a shine to Bryan and asked him: "*Would you like to come home with me?"* As has been stated, he was dimply and appealing, so I smiled my best smile – and despite voicing the fact that she really only wanted one evacuee, she took me too. Our brief time with her is marked by a few disconnected memories. Married, with two children, Mrs Hawkins seemed kind enough. I recall several appealing, yellow fluffy chicks chirping in a cardboard box which were kept in the warmth of the living room, and an alarming period of time when Bryan went missing for what seemed like a day but could have been two hours. He had borrowed Mrs Hawkins' son's bike (saddle missing, an old, tied on cushion in its place) and gone off to where I did not know. I had him mentally kidnapped, run over, and murdered in that short time for he did not know his away around and was only about seven years old! He later turned up safe and sound, grinning disarmingly, assuring me that - *I only wanted to find Sherwood Forest where Robin Hood comes from!* He'd thought that Nottingham was in Derbyshire and assumed it was just down the road apace. Of course, he never found the forest and probably only cycled a mile to the local park, but how he found his way home, I did not know! We were only in Mrs.Hawkins' care for a few weeks, when she decided that we were - '*Too much for me*!' Being polite, non-moronic children, I was puzzled as to why but, supposedly to her, we were no more than two pawns of war.

We didn't fare much better in our next foster home. Whilst our carers Mr. and Mrs.Ward may have meant well and were not unkind, it proved to be an unhappy stay.

On day one – the Ward's house was situated next door but one to a canal - a young evacuee boy fell in and sadly drowned. Not an auspicious start. The visiting mother of another child we knew, informed Mum of the tragedy and she bit her nails to the quick worrying about our safety thereafter. Because of the said nits, I had to have my curls cropped and was given a short back and sides which went down like a lead balloon, and our mealtime fare was not to our liking (particularly mine, although I kept my lips buttoned).

You can have either dripping or paste on bread for tea. And cake OR jelly.

There is a war on you know! announced our foster mother. Loving my food, and spoilt in that direction, I decided that rationing was an absolute pain. Mr Ward, a tall, well built man, kindly took us for walks along the narrow canal tow path of a Sunday morning. I believe that his intention was honourable! Mrs Ward, a whey-faced lady with her cap-like brown hair pulled in a tight roll to hug her neck and ears like an elongated turd, was a woman of serious demeanor. I can't recall her smiling much. One highlight of my stay, was meeting a friendly gypsy girl like a ray of sunshine called Chloe - frowned on by the Wards - who was part of a circus family visiting the area in a nearby park. She didn't lead me astray: our pleasure was the park swings and chatting. Bryan and I didn't like the sometimes luke-warm milk at school, yuch, and he got into trouble for paddling in a stream with his shoes and socks on. Talk in the house was on the hostile, negative side. Mrs. Ward moaned about:

The bad behaviour of the local Cockney evacuees. One lad broke Mrs Smith's grandfather clock, if you please. Little devils. And those two lads in the next street are always fighting!

I wasn't a Cockney, but felt like sticking up for them, as if they were close comrades.

Some of the local kids resented us and thought us intruders, picking fights. It wasn't always the evacuees' fault. Everything seemed out of sync. There were lots of niggling irritations. We made sure we watched our p's and q's. Down in the dumps, and homesick, we perked up when we heard that Aunt Doris was coming to visit and bringing no other than brother Terry, as Mum was pregnant and expecting a fourth sibling any day. We whooped with delight, and he seemed pleased to see us, whilst unimpressed about being sent away!

Conditions didn't improve any as Aunt Doris brought my stage clothes, and as I enrolled at a dancing school at Mum's suggestion and was due to appear in *"The Pied Piper of Hamlyn."* Beryl Ward, aged 10, turned into a green-eyed little monster. Bryan had to sleep on a mattress on the floor with his pillow on a high step to make room for Terry, and either he or Bryan – probably Bryan, Terry being even shyer – had a fight with the bad-tempered son of the house. My memories of Long Eaton are mixed ones as, apart from a lovely trip in the rolling hills and green countryside, the introduction to a cute, talking parrot belonging to a friend, and cavorting about at dancing class, the atmosphere in our foster home was marred by a miasma of gloom.

Fortunately, our stay wasn't a lengthy one for Aunt Doris - noticing how unhappy we were - and Dad, on leave, came and took us back to our old home in Dagenham once more, just before my third brother, Royce Kenneth, was born at the tail end of the war. I had learned about the Nomads in school and was beginning to wonder whether our family had Nomadic blood in its veins for, unbelievably, in a very short space of time, we were off again, after warmly welcoming our bonny new brother into the fold. Mum became quite unwell after his birth and was told to go *Somewhere quieter.*

The war wasn't letting us off the hook just yet! And so, once again, we packed our things, and along with Mum and the new addition to the family, plus her sister Peg and her brood, we relocated to Neath in South Wales.

The Germans seemed to be making one last, desperate statement in the shape of doodle bugs and rockets and anything else they could rain down on us. Aunt Sal had her own problems, bless her, for her ulcerated leg was giving her much pain, otherwise, we would have been welcomed back to Mountain Hare.

I have written elsewhere about our warm welcome to Neath. The family who took us in were admirable human beings. We felt wanted and safe staying in their midst for a short while. At last, with Mum recovered and the war on the brink of ending, we said a tearful goodbye to our harbouring family. I didn't reflect at the time as to how many thousands of rail miles we must have totted up during the war years, but it must have been something of a record! In my adult years, I have travelled a fair bit more, and moved numerous times. Although I am by nature quite a contented person, now and then I get a restless feeling to explore foreign territory. Even though I now live in Spain, and have done for nearly twelve years, I don't think that feeling will ever go away.

Another milestone for my memory, was brother Royce's christening in St. Peter's Catholic church. All the family were naturally invited, and squeezing into Grandma Rose's medium sized dining-room, wished for elasticated walls. Fortunately, the weather was good so we blessed the garden. Guest of honour that day was William (Bill) Boyle, Royce's American Godfather – a distant relative – a most likeable man, stationed in the UK and serving in the Air Force. Many years later, after marriage, my husband and I had the good fortune to stay with him and his lovely, hospitable, wife Mary in Brooklyn, New York. They took us to Staten Island and Coney Island – the latter quite unlike its movie image - and famous Central Park, en route to a brief life in Toronto, Canada.

PITMAN'S COLLEGE
& THE END OF THE WAR

HAVING ATTENDED A MOTLEY mix of schools until then, Mum decided it would be sensible if I attended Pitman's College in Forest Gate, London, to file away the many jagged edges of my education. I plumped for the mainstream course, which included French – which I embraced and enjoyed - when she had a re-think and suggested that I did the alternative commercial course instead, thereby learning shorthand and typing. I was sad to lose French lessons even though our French teacher (her face furnished with several warts) was quite a volatile person, while kind to me. A couple of our other teachers were decidedly odd. Our maths teacher - a small, insignificant man with teeth like small ancient tombstones - would stand over me and spray me with his vitriolic spittle as I was a duffer at maths. His balding pate was carefully – whilst not carefully enough – disguised with salt and pepper strands of greasy hair and he wore the same dirty beige raincoat for the duration of my schooling: about two and a half years. I became quite familiar with every gouge, knot and initial in the wood of the 'other side' of the classroom door. He had no patience with slow learners. My relationship with Mr Reginald, our Commerce and Book Keeping teacher, was an improvement, although he too had a short fuse and if the class was restless, he would bang his desk lid down with tremendous force and frighten the daylight from you, or close the windows on a warm/hot day if anyone dared talk or 'played up.' There was no air con.

198

then! With no 'Health & Safety' rules around... yet another teacher regularly threw the dangerous wooden blackboard eraser at pupils at will whenever he lost his temper, which was often. On one occasion he seriously hurt a friend called Edna, causing quite a kerfuffle!

Miss Jones - our English and Games teacher - was my favourite. She had an equable temperament and only ever told me off once for *Talking too much!* I adored reading *'Hiawatha'* and several other poems but found Shakespeare hard to understand at the time, falling in love with *'Hamlet' et al* decades later. I was undoubtedly a dreamer with a butterfly brain, and struggled through shorthand and typing, although my handwriting was impeccable and I was proud of my certificate.

Usually drawn to more dominant, bright and lively people, I sat up and took notice when a girl my own age starting 'holding court.' She was slender in build, with sparkling hazel-green eyes her best feature. Her face and body had an elfin quality and she attracted people like honey lures wasps. Her name is Sheila Smith, nee Devo and her outstanding attributes were - and still are - her bubbly personality and sense of humour and drama... It was no surprise that she later made an excellent secretary, landing many fascinating jobs - she was once secretary to Jack Hylton and a few other prominent impresarios - and graced many a stage with her admirable performances in several amateur productions. Many decades later – although we now live on different land masses and rarely see each other – we keep in touch and she remains an 'ever-young,' interesting and lively character. I had another friend in school for a while, but she later 'purloined' my boy friend at the time and married him, so I naturally spurned her friendship. That he was found to be a 'bounder' and divorced her was of some comfort!

Of course, nothing was as it should have been because of the war. There were ugly, weed-strewn gaps and bomb damaged buildings all over the place, disrupted journeys to and from school, and still the odd wailing air raid warning, although the war was in its death throes.

When peace was at long last declared, we were all ecstatic. The feared black-out disappeared in a blaze of lights. Theatres long used to gloomy exteriors, suddenly found themselves bathed in the brightest glow illuminating the pavements. Huge bonfires like beacons of hope, sprang up in many gardens and on waste ground, and our parents took my brothers and me to see the firework celebrations from a Westminster Bridge teeming with people whooping with delight, hugging, kissing, dancing and climbing lamp-posts, all inhibitions thrown to the wind. One newspaper reported:

'A huge 'V' sign glares down over Leicester Square. And crowds of girls and soldiers of all the allied nations are waving rattles and shouting in wild, happy, celebration mood.'

Mum's brother, our Uncle John – he of the *Perfect bottom for navy bell-bottoms*...happily left the Royal Navy to marry his pretty fiancé, nicknamed Bubbles because of her fair, curly hair and decided to become a Lighter-man, like Dad. Dad coached him as there was much to learn, more particularly memorising the bridges and their order, on which he would be tested by a Board of Examiners. A date was set for his exam and he was highly nervous so decided on a subtle move. He wore his naval uniform and went a step further by borrowing several medals and ribbons from Army and Air Force acquaintances. Fortunately, the elderly examiners' collective eyesight wasn't the sharpest, and one or two seemed visibly moved and approving. Dad reported them having shook their heads at sight of his proudly displayed 'fruit salad,' and the main spokesman said, after just a brief interrogation:

Enough questions, gentlemen, I think the poor lad's been through enough already. Uncle John announced it *A piece of cake!* Had he known about the initiation ceremony, he may not have felt quite so cocky, for it was said that all new Lighter-men's trousers were pulled around their ankles, and honey and feathers (or similar) and a large bow were applied to a sensitive part of their anatomy!!

Several days after the war in Europe's end, with celebrations over - a day when no enemy plane flew overhead, just one of ours – a Spitfire, Dad's favourite - and a kite riding the wind, I can recall skipping lightheartedly down the hill near our house. I wondered whether, in later years, I would remember that moment when our family was all together again, with Dad, one of the earliest conscripts to be demobbed, safe and sound, and dear Mum, cooking dinner in her own house as she used to, my heart full of pure happiness. Oh, I do!

201

War Note
In Dagenham alone, 190 people were killed, 1,627 injured and 25,252 houses damaged or demolished during the war years.

AFTER THE WAR

UNCLE BERNARD
AND MY FIRST AMOUR

IT IS SUMMER AND I am about to go on holiday from my school, Pitman's College. In nine months' time or so, I will be leaving to enter the world of commerce. My Godmother and companion on the trip, Aunt Doris, is in her late thirties and still unmarried. The second world war has ended. There is optimism in the air: undiluted joy for some folk, for others a vagueness of expression on their faces. A puzzled look, as if they have lost something or someone, which – of course – many have. Everyone is allowed to travel abroad again. It is my very first trip abroad.

Self conscious in my first 'New Look' grown-up clothes: soft, donkey brown wool dress with a cheeky 'peplum', suede and snakeskin (snakeskin!) and calf wedged, sling-backed shoes, my insides are acting in a strange manner. French fingers are beckoning on the other side of the English Channel. Another enigmatic adventure awaits!

Lurching violently from side to side in a dusty, battered black taxi, its driver oblivious of danger – we speed and bump over horrendous roads, ploughed up by tanks and trucks, mortars and machine-gun fire. We are in northern France: Merville to be exact, having traversed the calm waters of the English Channel on a ferry – the novel experience still blowing in my mind, like my hair on deck. Our destination is a farmhouse/café just outside of Merville town. The taxi treats us like pebbles in a drum and we clutch the door handles for dear life, fearful that our lunch will reappear. In between rows of cabbages and waving wheat, are green and earthy churned fields which yield mangled corpses and metallic entrails of German and British planes. Could one be the remains of Uncle Bernard's Blenheim 4 – bringing the war close again? We frighten cattle as we thunder by: I catch the fearful eye of a cow ...puts speed in the legs of a snoozing dog it didn't know it had. The few, forlorn, houses and farms we pass tell us of their recent history. All at once, with a jolt, catapulting us painfully forward, we are there. 'Fleur du Printemps' stands solidly before us, set in flat countryside as far as my eye can see - only some chipped and scuffed brick work, from shrapnel and blast waves - speaking of its fate. We are bowled over by a rapturous welcome. Clemence, my Dad's brief amour, stands at the door, her eyes dark as damsons, twinkling as they once did for her *Sharlie* (a secret to me then). She sweeps me up in a warm embrace, muttering *Oh, Sharlie's daughter!* elevating my humble position in the world. Two (Yolande and Annie) of her three daughters stand behind her, waiting to greet us. Also there are a thin, aged couple, she introduces as her parents. Smiles hover all around; hands are shaken, cheeks kissed: twice each time. I am overwhelmed; a little shy. Aunt Doris laps up the attention: a human butterfly with quick hand movements and an uncertain smattering of remembered school-girl French. Unsure, a blush on my cheeks, I stumble over my more recent knowledge of the language. Clemence, her thick jet-black hair cut short in a soft roll just under her ears, shocks me as she calls after the paid taxi driver: *Bastard!* (Did he over-charge?) He doesn't hear her. (Earlier, the Brits and Yanks were eager language tutors.) She tries a few more, tamer words in English, the meanings a bit jumbled and amusing.

Then clearly this time:

Your Mama – Lila. She is well? And your dear Papa, Sharlie? (is that a tear in her eye?) There is something in the air that I don't understand, a shifting of feet, a casting about of several pairs of eyes. Once inside the large main room of the café/farm, we are divested of our outer travelling clothes, seated and bade to eat. (Did my Dad sit in this very seat in 1939/40? Did he inhale the yeasty/spicy aroma, feel the heat from the central stove – novel with its flowered motif decoration - on his body?) A goose has been cooked in our honour: fatty but delicious, its accompaniments, except for a hearty salad, lost in the ether. Sweet, honeyed wafers and home-made jams are pressed upon us; glasses of red wine (over which I splutter to laughter). Aunt Doris is lenient…Clemence pinches my arm in several places, gently prods my stomach:

You too thin. I fatten you!

More sniggers. Lots of curious faces turn towards us, more exchanges of fractured English and French. We explore the outside: flat, brown earthy land, mainly farmed and green-stitched. It rolls away from us in acres. Several geese, necks outstretched, raucous at our approach, roam free.

We are shown the outside *Privies.* I imagine spiders, and pee while it's still light, hoping I can save the rest until morning. Dusk falls softly, the sky soon turning from darkening blue to black. Never have I seen so many stars.

Surely some impaled on spiky trees? We are shown our rooms. I am to sleep in a large one containing three beds: two single bedsteads and one curious double, with a set of wooden steps to reach the high mattress. There is a small dressing table and a large, looming dark wardrobe that threatens...At bedtime, I watch in fascination as *Grand-mere and Grand-pere* both in white nightshirts and nightcaps, climb the wooden stairs and try tucking each other in for the night. Shades of Dickens. Alas no wavering candles complete the image. Aunt Doris sleeps in another room nearby.

Tomorrow we will make a painful bicycle journey over cobbles to the local cemetery to look for the place where poor Uncle Bernard's body is, hopefully, laid to rest. The aroma of fresh coffee draws us to the kitchen this first morning like a magnet. More a novelty in the UK then, it proves delicious, made from fresh beans, ground before us, and served with cream. Croissants, another first, spread with butter and blackcurrant conserve, send my lip corners heaven ward. The kitchen smells like all kitchens should: edible.

After careful directions, we mount our bikes and are off, and soon the vibrations are resounding throughout my body (cobbles? Boulders more like!) After seeming miles, the cemetery gates, large and impressive, not too soon... greet us. Relief floods through me! A tall gentleman in long flowing black robes approaches us and speaks in fair English to my Aunt, directing us to a specific area in the churchyard. We park our bikes and a huge sadness overtakes me as I pass impressive and simple graves, noting the dates of the occupants' deaths. Too many younger than I, some the same age. Other graves bear elaborate, gilt-framed, pictures of the deceased. The layout of the cemetery and the grandness of some tombs and edifices have me gawping. Angels of giant proportions hover over loved ones, some bereft of wing, or limb. There are doves of peace and glass-domed artificial, garish flowers. A few foreign bodies lie in foreign soil. We scan the headstones, but nowhere can we find Uncle Bernard's last resting place. I imagine him floating forever in the English channel, or the North sea and cry briefly. Aunt Doris is deeply disappointed. Somehow or other, she convinced herself that she would find the grave of her youngest brother in this particular cemetery. I find this strange. Why, out of all the cemeteries in France, should he be buried here? Then I remember that Dad was stationed nearby, close to a former V2 rocket launching site (which, abandoned and eerily quiet, we later explored), built after he left for evacuation from Boulogne. We later learned that Clemence would pray the rockets wouldn't hit *Sharlie* or his family. But Dad was a "plane movement plotter," and his youngest brother an airborne sergeant/navigator, serving with 236 Sqn.Coastal Command (his last flight in a Blenheim 4) so it is odd that she links the two. They are located in totally different places and Uncle Bernard's plane was probably shot down over water. Like his body, she cannot put her mind to rest. We return to Clemence's warm welcome in low spirits.

Aunt Doris and I next visit the town of Lille; the wooden-seated train shows our derrieres no mercy...but our fellow passengers are curious and gossipy-friendly, the market there pungent with nose pleasing aromas: oranges and arum lilies, invoking thoughts of Christmas and weddings. A visit to a strange cinema in Merville town becomes a reality: bench seats, the film a jumble in my head, and during the interval, wine and cigarettes. Youngsters my age smoke in sophisticated style, and sip from their glasses as if to the manner born. I am introduced to *Paul* (maybe sixteen/seventeen), impish under a head of curly fair hair. He appraises me under thick lashes, smiles and speaks in clipped English. I blush and stammer in clumsy French. He then studies me openly, sits close, very upright, head inclined, edging even closer and acting, maybe twenty? Perspiration marks my palms. Aunt Doris doesn't notice, is chatting to someone. When the lights dim again, Paul kisses me quickly on one cheek, blows me a kiss and departs to join his friends. I am "all at sea" as they say, but flattered. When the film ends, he sidles up to me (he knows Clemence) and says: *I will write, cherie!* and kisses a hand. Aunt Doris notices and raises an eyebrow. I feel nervous and gauche. There is a P.S. at a later date. Aunt Doris and I visit Clemence's relatives: a cosy, smokey and coffee-impregnated cottage remains welcoming; faces a blur. Our hostess continues to prod and fatten, especially me. We stroll down country lanes, say *Bonjour* to strangers, and – come the day of our departure – are given a plucked goose wrapped in greased paper and tea cloths to give to *My dear Sharlie and Lila!*

Back in England, the postman brings me a letter with a French post mark a week later and several more thereafter. My Aunt helps me translate and is a little shocked at the passionate tones. *Paul is only seventeen after all!* Another eyebrow is raised. I write a few times in imperfect French.

Then a letter from Clemence herself. Aunt Doris tells me –

You must stop writing to Paul. He has stolen his grandmother's savings and had to be stopped from catching the ferry to England to see you.

At fourteen I was being wooed as if a heroine in a French novel! I tried looking shocked but was secretly pleased and all a-twitter at Paul's ardour. My first would-be amour. How romantic! How exciting. The fact that he was a thief seemed a trifling matter!

Aunt Doris and Grandma still lament the death of their brave, young airman. Several painted, model aeroplanes still dangle from the ceiling of his former bedroom; the half-hooked rug he was making stored in a cupboard. Has anyone married Uncle Bernard's last, sad, sweetheart?

Grandma Rose has never worn black. May he rest in peace.

Oh the puzzling juxtaposition of every-day events, the ordinary, the extraordinary and the tragedies in life!

About the Author

Along with an impressive array of letters, articles, poems and short stories published both in the UK and Spain, Joy Lennick has also seen two of her factual books appear in print (in the UK) plus a book of poems. More recently, she acted as biographer for Andrew Halsey's "Hurricane Halsey." An epileptic, he conquered the Atlantic in his rowing boat and challenged the might of the Pacific Ocean.

Joy won the First Short Story competition held in Torrevieja, Spain, in 2005 and acted as one of the judges for subsequent competitions. Since then, she has worked in close conjunction with WordPlay, of whom she is an ardent fan. Joy, who is married to Eric and has three sons, has "plenty of material on the back burner," and 2013 will see more of her work published.

Also written by Joy Lennick
Factual:
Running Your Own Small Hotel
Jobs in Baking and Confectionary
Biography
Hurricane Halsey (as biographer)
Poetry
Celtic Cameos & Other Poems

OTHER BOOKS PUBLISHED BY WORDPLAY

Fallyn and the Dragons
by K J Rollinson

Three children are taken from their dreams to rescue the people of Nashta from the evil Prince Bato. To do so, Fallyn and his friends must learn to ride the island's dragons, and use them in a war that threatens their return to the real world.

Words on the Wild Side
by Georgia Varjas

Known on the performance poetry scene as a verbal volcano, the inventive and incisive Georgia Varjas has collected eighty of her vibrant poems in a single book that will make you think about modern life in a whole new way.

Losing Hope
by Nikki Dee

In 1995 a small girl vanished from her home. No trace of her was found though her family never stopped looking. In 2010 a damaged and vulnerable young woman is rescued from a burning building. Can this possibly be that long lost child and, if so, where has she been and why?

The Cardinals of Schengen
by Michael Barton

Jack Hudson, the UK Government's Foreign Secretary, is assassinated in his own home. In attempting to discover his brother's murderer, Peter Hudson finds himself in a race against time to save Europe from a secret society determined to see Europe become the Fourth Reich.

WordPlay ShowCase
by Various Authors

A collection of works by a series of writers, for some of whom this represents their first time in print. The anthology covers a whole range of writing: factual, fiction, social commentary, and poetry.

COMING SOON FROM WORDPLAY

Fallyn in the Forbidden Land
by K J Rollinson

A magical adventure that sees Allan, Eileen and Martin called away from the 'real world' to a medieval 'dream world'. There Allan is known as Lord Fallyn, and he and his friends go to the rescue of King Rudri's dragons and battle against Prince Bato who seeks to depose his brother.

Looking Back, Walking Forward
by Ian Alexander and Joy Lennick

This is a thought provoking, yet often funny story detailing the trials and tribulations of a man and a woman in search of happiness within their respective relationships, cleverly told from the points of view of the protagonists in alternate chapters.

Precinct 25
by Various Authors

25 stories, 25 murders, each taking 25 minutes to read. For those that like their New York killings potted, this is the perfect coffee table crime anthology.

Blowback
by Michael Barton

Peter Hudson returns in this tale of political intrigue that sees Britain's criminal masterminds linking with government ministers determined to make their fortune by cornering the illegal drugs trade

Keep Write On
by Ian Govan

Published posthumously, *Keep Write On* is a collection of Ian's musings on life and, in particular, writing. There is wit, tinged with, perhaps, a little life cynicism here and there, that will make you giggle inside. All royalties from sales will be used by WordPlay toward 'encouraging writers to write, and then getting them read'.

7030637R00119

Printed in Great Britain
by Amazon.co.uk, Ltd.,
Marston Gate.